Africa Bible Commentary Series

Series Editors

Old Testament

Dr Nupanga Weanzana

New Testament

Dr Samuel Ngewa

Series Advisors

Solomon Andria, Tewoldemedhin Habtu, Samuel Ngewa

This commentary is written in a "sermon" or a "pastoral letter" style and blended with exegetical insights and life experiences. It proceeds by intertextual reading in order to interpret 2 Peter and Jude and then the author applies the teaching of these two books to denounce false teaching and malpractices rambling in prosperity gospel churches and traditional religions in Africa. This book presents evangelical traditions that balance other Christian and religious traditions found in Africa. It is a welcome building block for the consolidation of the unity and diversity of the church in Africa, and those of African biblical scholarship.

Jean-Claude Loba Mkole, PhD
Global Translation Adviser, United Bible Societies, Kenya

Africa Bible Commentary Series

2 PETER AND JUDE

Dieudonné Tamfu

HIPPOBOOKS

Published 2018 by HippoBooks, an imprint of ACTS and Langham Publishing.

Africa Christian Textbooks (ACTS), TCNN, PMB 2020, Bukuru, 930008, Plateau State, Nigeria.
www.actsnigeria.org

Langham Publishing (a ministry of Langham Partnership), PO Box 296, Carlisle, Cumbria, CA3 9WZ, UK.
www.langhampublishing.org

ISBNs:
978-1-78368-460-1 Print
978-1-78368-461-8 ePub
978-1-78368-462-5 Mobi
978-1-78368-463-2 PDF

British Library Cataloguing-in-Publication Data
A catalogue record for this book is available from the British Library.

ISBN: 978-1-78368-460-1

Cover & Book Design: projectluz.com
Cover art: Faces, 90 cm by 190 cm (size); black Afara (standard name of wood) or Ofram (local trade name of wood); 2006 by Elias Nanor of Ronan Collections, AB 425, Akosombo, Ghana. All rights reserved. Used with the artist's permission.

To Dominique M. Tamfu
who has obtained a faith of equal standing with me by the
righteousness of our God and Saviour Jesus Christ.

CONTENTS

2 PETER

JUDE

INTRODUCTION TO AFRICA BIBLE COMMENTARY SERIES

The church of Christ in Africa rejoiced at the launch of the Africa Bible Commentary (ABC) in 2006. This one-volume commentary was unique in being a product of African soil. Seventy African scholars representing many countries and denominations contributed commentaries on each of the sixty-six books of the Bible as well as articles on various themes of relevance to the African context.

But even as the ABC was being released, the ABC Board was looking ahead. A one-volume commentary does not provide enough space to deal with many important issues. Thus was born the Africa Bible Commentary Series.

This series provides more depth of study, width of explanation, and variety of application than was possible in the ABC. The contributors are Anglophone or Francophone African scholars, all of whom adhere to the statement of faith of the Association of Evangelicals in Africa.

Besides the African authorship, there are a number of other features that make this commentary series distinctive. First, each commentary is divided into preaching units to help pastors develop a series of sermons on that particular book of the Bible. The main text deals with issues that could come up in such a series, while more complex academic issues relating to the original languages and academic controversies are discussed in the comprehensive endnotes. Each unit ends with questions that can be used to stimulate discussion of the themes in that unit. Each book in the series also contains a number of case studies and brief articles expanding on the practical application of points mentioned in the text.

It is hoped that this combination of features will make these books valuable to pastors, students, and small group Bible study leaders, as well as to ordinary Christians who are interested in getting a fuller understanding of God's Word.

The Africa Bible Commentary Series is published under the HippoBooks imprint, named in honour of the great African theologian Augustine of Hippo. This imprint is governed by the ABC board placing ownership in the hands of Africans and is supported through Langham Partnership who help to disseminate the work widely and affordably.

The general editor for the New Testament series is Dr. Samuel Ngewa of the Nairobi Evangelical Graduate School of Theology (NEGST), Kenya, while the editor for the Old Testament series is Dr. Nupanga Weanzana of Bangui Evangelical School of Theology (BEST), in Bangui, Central African Republic.

The main goal of The Africa Bible Commentary Series is to relate the best biblical scholarship to the African context. This is no easy task. May the Lord bless the work of our hands and use it to strengthen his church in Africa. May our words also bring insight and encouragement to our fellow believers around the world.

Samuel Ngewa

FOREWORD

The Bible is wealth for the poor, food for the hungry, water for the thirsty, and light for those in darkness. God has spoken. The biblical authors were borne along by the Holy Spirit. The book of books reveals the Lord. I am so thankful that Dieudonné Tamfu has written this commentary on 2 Peter and Jude. This study can guide you through these parts of God's word, functioning as a key that unlocks the treasure, an invitation to the feast, a path to the river of living water, a switch that turns on the light.

In these pages you will find a patient and careful examination of the text of Scripture that throbs with Spirit-wrought passion for God, his word, and his people. There are knotty interpretive questions in 2 Peter and Jude, and this study shrinks from none of the difficulties. Complexities are acknowledged, evidence examined, and sane interpretations expounded with clear-headed vigour.

God's people need God's word. Those who shepherd God's people need to understand what the biblical authors have written, and we need to be able to explain it to others. If you are called to the most noble work of teaching God's word to God's people, when the time comes to exposit 2 Peter and Jude, I commend this book to you. Your thinking will be stimulated and stretched by the close reading of the text reflected in these pages.

May the Lord use his word "to keep you from stumbling and to present you blameless before the presence of his glory with great joy" (Jude 24).

James M. Hamilton Jr.
Professor of Biblical Theology
Southern Baptist Theological Seminary
Louisville, Kentucky

ACKNOWLEDGEMENTS

I write this commentary for pastors, lay leaders, and Christians who are serious about studying the Bible. My hope is that God will use it to increase your joy in Christ and your grasp of the Scriptures. To this end, I have attempted to include as many Scripture references as possible to encourage further exploration.

Working on this commentary while a full-time PhD candidate at the Southern Baptist Theological Seminary in Louisville, KY, in the United States of America was challenging. God used several people to cheer me along the way. Dr Daniel M. Gurtner, by whose effort I was granted the opportunity to write this commentary, constantly prayed for me and emailed me to cheer me and remind me why I was doing this work. I thank God for Adrien and Richard Segal, my "parents" who have not only prayed and encouraged me, but have sacrificed financially by paying for my studies so that I could devote time to work on this commentary and do my school work without any distractions. Many friends have partnered with me financially as well, for whom I will always be grateful. Craig Howse, my grandma Regina Tangiri, and many others constantly prayed that God would use this work to advance the cause of Christ.

My wife Dominique was a source of immense encouragement to me in the process. She read through 2 Peter and Jude and compiled questions that proved remarkably helpful to me as I wrote. Her love has been a soothing, heart-calming, burden-lifting gift of God. I can say confidently that without her presence in my life, this commentary could not have been what it is.

I am thankful to Dr James M. Hamilton, my PhD supervisor, who took time out of his busy schedule to read through this commentary and write the foreword. I will always be indebted to his scholarship.

I also deeply appreciate the work of Isobel Stevenson of Langham Partnership, without whose editorial help this commentary would not be what it is. The remaining weaknesses are due to my own human limitations.

Ultimately, it was the power of God's precious promises that sustained me through the process of writing. His grace kept me in his love throughout. I give all the glory to God for his kindness and it is my prayer that all who read this work will be changed by the power of God's promises and partake in his divine nature.

ABBREVIATIONS

Books of the Bible

Old Testament (OT)

Gen, Exod, Lev, Num, Deut, Josh, Judg, Ruth, 1–2 Sam, 1–2 Kgs, 1–2 Chr, Ezra, Neh, Esth, Job, Ps/Pss, Prov, Eccl, Song, Isa, Jer, Lam, Ezek, Dan, Hos, Joel, Amos, Obad, Jonah, Mic, Nah, Hab, Zeph, Hag, Zech, Mal

New Testament (NT)

Matt, Mark, Luke, John, Acts, Rom, 1–2 Cor, Gal, Eph, Phil, Col, 1–2 Thess, 1–2 Tim, Titus, Phlm, Heb, Jas, 1–2 Pet, 1–2–3 John, Jude, Rev

Modern Translations

ESV	English Standard Version
KJV	King James Version
LXX	The Septuagint
NASB	New American Standard Bible
NEB	The New English Bible
NET	New English Translation
NIV	New International Version
NKJV	New King James Version
NLT	New Living Translation
RSV	Revised Standard Version

Commentary Series

ACCS	Ancient Christian Commentary on Scripture
BNTC	Baker New Testament Commentary
BST	Bible Speaks Today
CBC	Cornerstone Biblical Commentary
ICC	International Critical Commentary
NAC	New American Commentary
NIVAC	NIV Application Commentary
TNTC	Tyndale New Testament Commentary
WBC	Word Biblical Commentary

Journals

EvRT	*Evangelical Review of Theology*

2 PETER

INTRODUCTION

When an African father knows that he is at death's door, he gathers his sons around him to hear his will and receive his final instructions. Most of what he has to say may not be new to them, but he needs to re-emphasize things he has told them in the past. He warns them about what to avoid and gives them advice on how to share the inheritance and live their lives. Because he is on his deathbed, he expects them to pay close attention and carry out all his instructions. His last words to his sons carry considerable weight because of their timing, content, and purpose.

In many respects, 2 Peter is like the words a dying father utters on his deathbed. As regards timing, these were the last words that Peter would speak to his spiritual children. As regards content, he did not write to tell believers new things but to remind them of what he and the other apostles had taught them. As regards his purpose, Peter wanted the believers to stay true to the faith after his demise. To keep them from straying, he warned them against false teaching that was casting doubts on the hope of Christ's return and promoting immorality.

Authorship and Date

Not everyone accepts that 2 Peter was actually written by the Apostle Peter. Some scholars argue that it was written by someone living in the second century AD, using Peter's name but with no intention to deceive because his readers would know what he was doing.[1] Their reasons for thinking that Peter could not have written 2 Peter are related to the style of the Greek and the content of the letter.[2] However, the letter itself gives three reasons why it should be regarded as coming from the apostle:

- He is explicitly named as the author in 1:1.

- According to 3:1, this letter was written by the same person who wrote 1 Peter, which is generally accepted as coming from the apostle.[3]

- The author claims to have been an eyewitness to what happened on the Mount of Transfiguration (1:13–16). This means that he must be either Peter, James or John (Matt 17:1–9). Since Peter is the one named at the start of this letter, it must come from his hand.

Based on these internal evidences, we can say with some level of confidence that the Apostle Peter wrote this letter.[4]

When did he write it? We know that it was written shortly before Peter's death as he explicitly says that the time of his departure (death) is near (1:13–14). Given that he probably died during Emperor Nero's persecution of Christians in Rome, it is likely that this letter was written sometime between AD 60 and AD 68.

Just as our respect for our fathers affects our response to their words on their deathbed, so our respect for the Apostle Peter should shape our reception of this letter, which he wrote at the end of his life. His words carry apostolic authority, which is in essence Christ's authority, and are as relevant to us as the rest of Scripture.

As you study this letter, will you submit to what the apostle of Christ says to you or will you reject his words, which are the words of Christ? I urge you to receive the content of this letter as what it really is, the very word of the Messiah for you (see also 1 Thess 2:13). Just as children honour a father's wishes after he is dead and gone, so we should honour Peter's words and value them as a guide to life.

Structure of the Letter

Peter dedicated his last words to guarding his readers from false teaching and guiding them in the truth. He embeds his purpose in the very structure of the letter, as you can see from the following diagram.[5]

1:1–15 Make every effort to grow in grace, knowledge, and virtue

1:16–21 Hold fast to the apostolic teaching about the return of Christ

2:1–22 False teachers identified and denounced

3:1–13 Hold fast to the apostolic teaching about the return of Christ

> 3:14–18 Make every effort to grow in the grace and knowledge
> of Christ

When we look at this structure, we can see that Peter begins and ends his letter with references to the grace and knowledge of God and commands the believers to "make every effort" to grow in these things (1:1–15; 3:14–18).[6] This structure reveals one of his aims. On his deathbed, his greatest desire is that his spiritual children would become mature by growing in their understanding and practice of godliness. They need to do this so that they can resist the false teaching that undermines moral living and misrepresents Christ and his second coming, leading some to completely reject Christ (2:1). So in 1:16–21 and 3:1–13 Peter directs the believers to the apostolic teaching, urging them to hold fast to the truths that he and the other apostles taught them.

We still need to pay attention to those truths today. False teaching is spreading like wildfire, and we must return to the ancient apostolic teaching if we are to grow in grace and in true knowledge of Christ and so outshine the darkness of ancestral worship, the health and wealth gospel, syncretism, and all the other sins that are suffocating the church in Africa.

Looking at the diagram above, you can see that at the centre of the letter (2:1–22) Peter directly addresses the false teaching that was trying to draw the believers away from true doctrines. The false teachers were denying the second coming of Christ and twisting Scripture to support their views (1:20–21; 3:15–16). Although they did not explicitly reject apostolic authority, Peter interprets their repudiation of the return of Christ and final judgement as equivalent to a rejection of apostolic authority (3:3–4).[7]

Given the nature of the false teaching, it is not surprising that in this letter Peter focuses on eschatology and final judgement (1:16–3:13).[8] He reminds his readers that God will judge the impure, and so they must conduct themselves in a manner worthy of their calling, as they wait for the day of judgement.

The challenge that comes to each of us is whether we are ready to face the final judgement. Ready yourself by trusting in Jesus for your salvation, rather than in false gods. African deities cannot condemn you forever, but the God of the Bible will do so in the final judgement if you do not repent and turn to Jesus for the salvation of your soul.

AUTHORSHIP AND BLESSING

In Cameroon a local chief who wants to send a message to the community may choose to delegate his authority to a messenger who would speak on his behalf. He confirms that this person is his spokesman by giving him a staff or some other symbolic object to hold when delivering the message. This object represents the chief's authority. The one who carries such a staff or symbolic object must be treated with the same respect as would be shown to the leader himself, for he carries the authority of the chief as he speaks for the chief and delivers the chief's message.

Just as the messenger sent by a chief speaks for the chief, so the writer of this letter identifies himself as speaking for Christ, with the authority of Christ. In other words, what Peter says in this letter is a message from Christ, and as we listen to what Peter has to say, we are listening to Christ.

1:1a The Author

The author of the letter identifies himself in three ways: by his name Simon Peter, by his role as a servant of Christ, and by his role as an apostle.

Simon Peter

Simon was Peter's personal name[9] and *Peter* was the Greek form of the name Jesus gave him in Mark 3:16. In Aramaic, this name was Cephas (see John 1:42; 1 Cor 1:12; 3:22; 9:5; 15:5; Gal 1:18; 2:9, 11, 14). Peter was a fisherman (Mark 1:16; Luke 5:2–3, 9–10; John 21:3) and the son of a man named Jonah (Matt 16:17). Like the other disciples, he was a sinner unworthy of Christ's holy presence (Luke 5:8). His uncleanness could not stand the light of the Holy One of God, Jesus Christ.

After Christ called Peter, he became a leader among the disciples. He could be self-sacrificing (Mark 1:18; Luke 5:11) and spiritually perceptive (John 6:68), but his faith was not always strong. He could also be presumptuous and proud (Matt 16:22; John 13:8; 18:10) and fearful (Matt 14:30). He was too inclined to please other people and so was sometimes hypocritical (Matt 26:69–72; Gal 2:11–14). He could be self-seeking (Matt 19:27) and slow to understand spiritual matters (Matt 13:36; 15:15–16). Even though he recognized that Jesus was the Messiah (Matt 16:16), he failed miserably when he denied Christ three times (Mark 14:71).

Yet despite all these flaws, after Jesus called him, and after he left everything and followed Jesus (Luke 5:9–11), Peter became one of the inner circle of the apostolic team (Mark 5:35–41; 9:2–8; 14:33, 43–50) and a leader (Matt 10:2; Mark 3:16; Luke 6:14) who spoke for the other disciples (Matt 17:24; Mark 8:29; Luke 12:41).

Christ's church was founded on Peter's confession of Jesus as the Messiah (Matt 16:16). Out of the sinner who was spring-loaded with inconsistencies, God made a preacher through whom thousands turned to the Lord (Acts 2:14–41). He performed miracles (Acts 3) and became as bold as a lion in the face of persecution (Acts 4:1–22; 5:12–40). He went on a missionary journey to Lydda and Joppa (Acts 9:32–43) and he was one of those whom God used to open the door of salvation to Gentiles (Acts 10). He played a prominent role in the church in Jerusalem that was led by James the brother of Jesus (Acts 15) and later became the apostle to the Jews (Gal 2:7–8). According to tradition, Peter died as a martyr in Rome during Nero's persecution. It is said that he was crucified upside down because he felt unworthy to die in the same way as Jesus his master.[10]

Peter's life demonstrates God's power to make something out of nothingness. If you consider yourself an unworthy sinner, trust Christ's cleansing blood and God will make something out of your nothingness for his glory, as he did in Peter.

Jesus changed Peter from a fisherman to one who fished for people and revealed to him majestic glory that none of the other disciples except James and John ever saw (Matt 17:1–8; Mark 9:2–8; Luke 9:28–36). Eyes that were once unworthy to look on Jesus beheld the eye-blinding, majestic, divine glory of Christ (2 Pet 1:16).

If you feel unworthy, do not run away; draw near to Christ. All he requires is that you see your need of him. "If you linger till you're better, you will never come at all."[11] Peter heard the call and was transformed from a sinner to a servant. Will you also hear Christ's call and be transformed?

A servant of Jesus Christ

It is striking, given Peter's leadership among the apostles and the glorious experiences he had with Christ, that when he introduces himself he does not describe himself as a great leader but as a servant ("bond slave" – NET; "bondservant" – NASB; "slave" – NLT). The Greek word he uses refers to someone whose life is controlled by another (see also Matt 8:9; John 13:16 and Col 4:1).[12] When Peter says he is *a servant of Jesus Christ*, he is declaring his total allegiance to Christ. He is not his own; he belongs to and lives for Christ. He has relinquished all his rights, and now he serves and submits to Christ in the same way that a houseboy would be expected to serve and submit to his master.

But the term "servant" does not only denote slavery. It is also a term of honour in the Old Testament, where it is used to refer to people with whom God had a special relationship because he had called them. Abraham, Moses, David and the prophets were servants (slaves) of God (Exod 32:13; Deut 34:5; 2 Sam 7:5; 2 Kgs 21:10). Moreover, Isaiah predicted that the coming Messiah would be the Servant of Yahweh par excellence (Isa 42:1–4; 49:1–6; 50:4–9; 52:13–53:12). Jesus as the Servant of God did not come to be served but to serve (Mark 10:45; John 13:4–5; Phil 2:7). He instructed his followers to be servants, not masters (Matt 10:24). So when Peter calls himself a servant of Jesus Christ, he is also identifying with Old Testament saints, following in the footsteps of his master, Jesus Christ, and obeying Christ's command.

What about you? Are you too proud to be called a servant? Do you insist on being called Reverend, Doctor, Bishop or some other honourable title? Learn from the Apostle Peter, and do not put your energy into seeking honour from other people. Remember that like him you are called to be Christ's humble servant.

For Peter, there is only one master, Jesus Christ, and Peter serves him alone since "no one can serve two masters. Either you will hate the one and love the other, or you will be devoted to the other and despise the other. You cannot serve both God and money" (Matt 6:24). Whom do you serve? Who is the master of your body, your mind, and your heart?

An apostle of Christ Jesus

Simon Peter also calls himself an *apostle*. The word "apostle" means "someone who is sent out" and so refers to a messenger. But an apostle is not just an ordinary messenger, like the office messengers who sort the mail and deliver parcels and documents to clients. An "apostle" is someone who is a special messenger handpicked for a particular mission.[13]

The word "apostle" first occurs in the New Testament when Jesus sends out twelve of his disciples to preach (Matt 10:2, 5–7; Mark 3:13; Luke 6:13). Their primary function was to "witness for Christ, based on years of intimate knowledge, experience, and training."[14] The apostles were messengers of Christ with the message of Christ, about Christ, and for Christ. As messengers, they had an extraordinary status based on the person they represented.[15] Just as an ambassador bears the authority of and represents the government of a country, so the apostles represented their master, Christ.

According to Jesus, both apostles and prophets are sent by God. And while both share this high honour, they both also share the same possible fate: "God in his wisdom said, 'I will send them prophets and apostles, some of whom they will kill and others they will persecute'" (Luke 11:49). Thus, when Peter identifies himself as an apostle, it indicates that in proclaiming Christ and sending this important letter to the church, he is risking his life.

1:1b The Audience and Their Faith

In his first letter, Peter was quite clear about whom he was writing to – they were "God's elect, exiles scattered throughout the provinces of Pontus, Galatia, Cappadocia, Asia, and Bithynia" (1 Pet 1:1). But in his second letter, he describes his readers in theological terms, without indicating where they are living. However, later in the letter, he does say, "this is now my second letter to you" (3:1), which suggests that he is writing to the same group to whom he directed his first letter. If so, they were probably Gentile Christians living in the Roman province of Asia, which today forms part of Turkey.[16] Like Christians in some parts of Africa today, these believers were suffering for their faith and encountering false teaching.

Listen to how Peter describes them. They are people "who through the righteousness of our God and Saviour Jesus Christ have received a faith as precious as ours" (1 Pet 1:1). These words highlight four important truths:

Faith is God's gift

The believers are said to have *received a faith*. Sometimes the New Testament speaks of "the faith", referring to an objective body of truth that is believed (1 Tim 3:9). But the faith Peter is speaking of here is not objective knowledge about God but subjective trust in God.[17] This faith does not only know about God; it depends on him. It is the powerful work of God in our hearts (Col 2:12). Moreover, this faith is not something that we have to work up in ourselves or something we have to earn: it is a gift of God. In African Traditional Religion, the gods are said to respond to requests on the basis of the merit of the one asking and the performance of the right rituals, but the God of the Bible gives generously to the undeserving because he is the God of all mercies. He is the one who grants faith (Phil 1:29; Eph 2:8; see also Acts 14:27). He does so by his own sovereign will. In fact the word translated "received" means "obtaining something by divine will or allotment".[18] Trust in God is, therefore, a gift of God and a powerful work of God in our hearts (see Col 2:12). Do you have this gift? Pray that God would give you faith to trust in his Son for salvation.

Faith is given equally to all believers

Peter states that his readers have received a faith *as precious as ours*. This is amazing. We live in societies where things are often very unequal. Some have many privileges and others have none. But God's grace "is open and accessible to all, which is to say to apostles and non-apostles."[19] Both groups have equal faith and equal standing before God. Although the apostles were with Christ, saw his glory, observed his miracles, and had many other privileges, their faith is no different from the faith that God gives to others. Apostles, preachers, pastors, bishops, Jews, Gentiles, rich and poor, young and old, black and white, educated and uneducated, the physically fit and the disabled, men and women of any race or nationality – all believers in Christ have received the same faith from God. There is no distinction, for we have the same faith, worship the same Lord, and have the same standing before God (see also Rom 10:12; Gal 3:28).

Faith comes through the righteousness of God

God gives faith *through the righteousness of our God and Saviour Jesus Christ*. What does this mean? It may mean that God is fair. This is the interpretation reflected in the NLT, which reads "this faith was given to you because of the justice and fairness of Jesus Christ". But the problem with that line of interpretation is that it suggests that God is like a judge who hears cases and then issues a decision on the basis of the evidence and the merit of the accused. But that is not how the New Testament presents the way God grants saving faith – he does not assign faith according to merit or because we can make a good case for why we deserve faith. Rather, he distributes faith freely (see Eph 2:8–9; Phil 1:29). So it is best to interpret this reference to God's righteousness in terms of the Old Testament where God's "righteousness" refers to his power to save. Look at Psalm 36:6:

> Your righteousness is like the highest mountains,
>   your justice like the great deep.
> You, LORD, preserve both people and animals.

The psalmist says that God shows his righteousness by saving both people and animals (see also Pss 35:24; 48:10; 51:14; 71:16, 19). If Peter is thinking in these terms, his point is that God freely grants equal faith to all believers by his saving power. We believe because of the working of his "incomparably great power for us" (Eph 1:19–20).

Jesus is God

Peter says that believers have obtained faith *through the righteousness of our God and Saviour Jesus Christ*. In English, this phrase could be interpreted as referring to two distinct beings, God and Jesus Christ. But that was not what Peter was saying. The Greek construction he uses clearly indicates that he is referring to only one person, Jesus, who is both our God and our Saviour.[20] So Peter implies that Jesus is God. The Apostle John also affirms the deity of Christ (John 1:1, 18; 10:30, 38; 20:28). So do other New Testament writers (Rom 9:5; Titus 2:13; Heb 1:8). The fact that Peter feels free to mention Christ's deity without any further explanation suggests that it was a common belief in the early church. It is by the saving power of our God and Saviour Jesus Christ that we have faith leading to salvation; we are not saved by our ancestors or the idols of African traditional religions.

By giving Jesus the title "Saviour", Peter is also associating him with Yahweh.[21] In the Old Testament Yahweh is the Saviour (Exod 3:7–8). He was Israel's saviour at the time of the Exodus (Exod 16:6, 32; 20:2),[22] David's saviour (2 Sam 22:3), and the saviour of those who seek him (Ps 17:7). Besides him there is no other saviour (Isaiah 43:3, 11; Hos 13:4). If Yahweh is the only Saviour in the Old Testament, then to call Jesus the Saviour is to say that he and Yahweh are one (see also John 10:30). This point is made even more strongly in the letter of Jude, which speaks of Jesus being the one who saved Israel from Egypt (Jude 5). The Israelites were saved from physical slavery, and now Jesus our God and Saviour has saved us from slavery to sin and Satan. In Christ we are on a new exodus to our heavenly home.

1:2 The Blessing

After introducing himself and theologically identifying his audience, Peter prays for his readers: *Grace and peace be yours in abundance through the knowledge of God and of Jesus our Lord.* "Grace" is God's unmerited favour to undeserving people. It is his gift. But we may be surprised to find that the word "grace" is also used in the context of a command in this letter. In 3:18 Peter commands his audience to grow in grace. Although God's grace is a gift, we also have the responsibility to flourish in it. Grace is a gift and those who share in this gift must grow in it through their growing knowledge of Christ.

The combination of *grace and peace* in Peter's blessing is theologically significant in that those to whom God has granted grace experience God's peace (see also 3:14). When Peter asks for peace, he is asking for the reconciling peace of God, which has broken down the hostility between God and sinners, to fill the hearts of the believers as they read his letter. This peace, whose source is God,[23] is not necessarily the same thing as peace of mind; rather, it is the settled conviction that one is reconciled with God. This peace is rooted in the fact that there is no hostility between God and those who are in Christ. If you are persecuted, trust God for his abundant grace and pray for his peace to guard your heart. Do not let persecution, pain, or any kind of distress steal this peace of God from you.

God multiplies grace and peace to us *through the knowledge of God and of Jesus our Lord* (see also 3:18). This phrase can be read in two ways: on the one hand, this knowledge is the knowledge we have about God and Jesus Christ, and on the other, it is knowledge that God and Jesus Christ give to us about themselves.[24] Both meanings apply here, since the only knowledge that brings grace is knowledge about God and Christ, and only God is the source of knowledge about God. Without divine revelation, we would have no hope of knowing God and Jesus. So we must "press on to know the LORD" (Hos 6:3 NRSV)[25] with humility, because he alone gives knowledge of himself (see also Prov 2:1–6; 2 Tim 2:7).

The knowledge about God that we get from God is the means by which God sends us his grace and peace. It has been said that "grace and peace abound when believers know more about God and come to know God in a deeper way in the crucible of experience."[26] Life's experiences, difficult as they may be, are one of the best means of growing in our knowledge of God. It is not enough to know the Bible; we need experience to drive that knowledge into our hearts. Through suffering, the death of a loved one, persecution, sickness and pain, God trains those whose faith is set on Christ to know him more fully, love him more dearly, and walk more closely with him.

Questions for Discussion

1. Peter states that the knowledge of God is the means by which God gives grace and peace to us. In what ways can we seek to increase our experiential as well as our intellectual knowledge of God?

2. Many who claim to speak for God promise people wealth, health, and a peaceful life in this present age. Would you consider such preachers true servants of God like Peter? Why or why not? Consider Jeremiah 23:16–17, 27–29.

THE TRANSFORMING POWER OF GOD'S PROMISES

Promises have the power to transform. I recently conducted a wedding and watched and listened as my dear friends exchanged their vows, promising to commit themselves to serving one another for all their days. A few weeks later, I visited the couple to check-in on how things were going. One of the first things I heard was that saying "I do" changes things significantly. Not only were they having more conflicts than they had ever imagined, but, more importantly, they were also finding joy in each other in ways they would never have imagined. The promises they had made to each other on their wedding day had transformed their relationship so much that neither of them would ever be the same again.

Just as wedding vows (promises) transform a couple, so God's promises transform those who embrace them. So Peter, writing to believers who are being battered by false teaching, reminds them that they must not trust the false promises being made by perfidious preachers (see 2 Pet 2:19) but must instead trust in the life-changing promises of God.

1:3 Christ's Power

Those who have been drawn to God and have received the gift of faith and the knowledge of God know that they need to live godly lives. But how do we go about doing this? We know from experience that godliness cannot be manufactured by human effort.

Peter knows that our only hope of transformation lies beyond ourselves in God. He explains this in 1:3–4 (which is all one long and complicated sentence in the original Greek).[27] His opening words are *his divine power* (1:3).

But immediately we have a question: Who does the pronoun "his" refer to – Christ or God the Father? Given that the previous sentence ended with a reference to "Jesus our Lord", the natural interpretation is that Peter is speaking about Christ. So when Peter speaks of *his divine power*, he is saying that Christ has the power of deity.[28] Divine power implies Christ's deity. We may not find this surprising, for African Traditional Religion has accustomed us to thinking of all sorts of spiritual powers. But we must not forget that Peter was Jewish, and for the Jews there was only one divine figure, the God of the Bible. It is an amazing and impressive testimony that a Jewish apostle implies that Christ, the one who is wielding this divine power, is God!

What is Christ doing with his divine power? He is using it to give *us everything we need for a godly life* (1:3a). Note that in using the pronouns "us" and "we" Peter is not referring just to himself and the small group of apostles. He is speaking of something that all Christians get, just as in 1:1 he said that both apostles and ordinary Christians have been given the same faith. Christ's power is not just for the elite but for everyone who truly believes in him.

What is amazing is that he gives us *everything we need*. I can think of so many things I need – a bigger house, a better car, money for my son's education . . . the list goes on and on. But my dreams hit a roadblock when I read the complete sentence. We are being promised *everything we need for a godly life* – which is not to be confused with getting everything we want. God may never give us some of the things we crave, but he will not fail to provide what we truly need to live godly lives (Phil 4:19).

However, any disappointment we feel at not getting some of the things we want fades away when we start to think about what God has promised us, and more especially when we look at Peter's exact words in the Greek text, which are accurately reflected in the ESV translation, which speaks of everything we need for "life and godliness".

The "life" Peter is referring to is eternal life. We sometimes think of "eternal life" as starting after we die. But the New Testament says that our eternal life begins as soon as we trust in Jesus for salvation (see John 3:15, 16, 36; 5:24). We already have eternal life, and so we had better start resting in it, with the help of Christ.

"But", you may say, "I thought eternal life was supposed to be blissfully happy, and my current life certainly isn't." But eternal life is not only an experience of bliss; it also requires moral transformation – that is why Christ's power gives us what we need for "life and godliness". We cannot have eternal life without godliness for, as the writer of the letter to the Hebrews reminds us, "without holiness no one will see the Lord" (Heb 12:14 NIV).

Jesus himself defines eternal life as an intimate relationship with God and Christ: "Now this is eternal life: that they know you, the only true God, and Jesus Christ whom you have sent" (John 17:3). Based on this definition, to have eternal life is to grow in an intimate, relational knowledge of God and Christ. God has given us all that we need for a life-changing knowing of God and Christ, and so we should invest our lives in growing our intimate knowledge of Christ, by which we will be transformed into greater Christ-likeness.

What does "godliness" mean?[29] In the simplest terms, it means becoming like God. Think, for example, of how young people show their admiration for someone. If their hero always wears a suit, they want to wear a suit. If she wears flashy jewellery, or braids her hair in a certain way, her admirers will try to copy the same look. In a somewhat similar way, Christians should start to "look like God" – not just because we are copying "the look" but because we have been given the power to become like him. Which brings us back to our earlier point: Christ does not exercise his divine power to meet our cravings; rather, his power is put to work to make us more like him, so that we too "may participate in the divine nature" (1:4 NIV).

How does Christ go about giving us what we need for eternal life and a holy life? Peter's answer is that he does it *through our knowledge of him who called us* (1:3b), that is, through our knowledge of God, the one who sent Christ and called us (1:2, 3; see also John 17:3). This "knowledge" involves much more than just knowledge about God to which we give mental assent; it is the knowledge that comes from having a close relationship with God. We get an idea of how intimate this relationship is when we read the book of Hosea, in which God says to his people, "I will betroth you to me in faithfulness. And you shall know the LORD" (Hosea 2:20 ESV).[30] The knowledge of God that Peter is speaking of can be compared to the way a woman knows her husband. This goes far beyond mere intellectual knowledge about who he is; it shapes the way she lives. It is only when we have this type of life-transforming knowledge of God that we experience his grace and peace (1:1) and his power at work in us.

But, some of you may say, couldn't the "him" in the phrase "him who called us" refer to Jesus, rather than God?[31] Certainly, it could, although it is more likely that it refers to God the Father, for in the New Testament the Father is usually the one who calls (see Rom 9:24; 1 Thess 4:7; 2 Tim 1:9). But in practice it makes little difference whether the "him" refers to God or Christ, for both are divine and knowledge of one means knowledge of the other – a point that was driven home in 1:1 where Peter referred to "the knowledge of God and of Jesus our Lord".

What does it mean to say that God has "called" us? Today, we sometimes speak of someone's "calling" as their occupation. They may be called to be a preacher or a doctor. But that is not the sort of calling that is being spoken of here. What Peter is speaking of is the calling that every Christian has received, namely God's call to come to him for salvation. Paul tells us that this calling guarantees our justification and glorification (Rom 8:30). According to 1 Peter, God called believers out of darkness (1 Pet 2:9) into his eternal glory in Christ (1 Pet 5:10), so that they may be holy as he who called them is holy (1 Pet 1:15), and live to proclaim his excellence (1 Pet 2:9).

God's calling came *by his own glory and goodness* (1:3c). The Greek preposition translated as "for" can also mean "to" and "by". Let us address each of these possible and acceptable translations one at a time. First, "for": God called us "*for* his own glory and goodness" (or "excellence" in the ESV). God did not call us without an aim; rather, he called us for a specific purpose, namely, to display his glory and his brilliance.[32] This interpretation is supported by 1 Peter 2:9, which reads, "You are a chosen people, a royal priesthood, a holy nation, God's special possession, that you may declare the praises of him who called you out of darkness into his wonderful light" (NIV). The word translated "praises" in this verse is the same word translated "goodness" in 2 Peter 1:3, which is why many English versions render it as "excellence", a word that has a wider scope than just "goodness". The calling out of darkness into the light described in 1 Peter 2:9 reminds us not of God's moral goodness but of the glorious moment when God called light into existence out of the darkness that was over the face of the deep (Gen 1:2–3). Just as God displayed his glory in the original creation (see Ps 19:1), so he is now displaying his glory by calling us out of the darkness of sin and making us into a new creation in Christ. His glory and greatness are the goal of our salvation.

Second, we would not be wrong to translate the phrase as referring to God's calling us "*to* his own glory and goodness" (ESV, KJV, RSV).[33] After all, God saves us so that we can "participate in the divine nature" (1:4 NIV) and in 1:5 we are told to cultivate "goodness" – and here again the same word is used as in 1:3. As we get to know God, we are to become like him (see Phil 4:8). As we look to Christ, we become like the one we are looking at and come to share his glory and goodness (see 2 Cor 3:18).

Finally, we come to the translation favoured by the NIV, namely that God called us "by his own glory and goodness". This translation suggests that God calls unbelievers by opening their eyes to see his splendour and moral excellence.[34] Paul makes a similar point when he writes, "For God, who said, 'Let light shine out of darkness,' has shone in our hearts to give the light of the knowledge of the glory of God in the face of Jesus Christ" (2 Cor 4:6 ESV). When the light of God shines in our hearts, we perceive God's glory in the face of Jesus, and that is how we are recreated in Christ.

We can summarize all that we have been saying in this section like this: Christ's divine power gives his people all that they need to become like him by giving them knowledge of God so that they in turn can share in and show what God is like. What an amazing honour! And what a responsibility!

1:4 God's Promises

Peter now goes on to show that all that he has been saying about the power of God at work in us is rooted in the *very great and precious promises* of God (1:4a). These promises, too, are rooted in God's glory and goodness, for the pronoun "these" in the NIV refers to his "glory and goodness" in verse 3.[35] Thus God's power, his goodness and his promises are all related. In humans, power, goodness and promises are often separate: the powerful make promises that have less to do with their goodness than with their desire to be re-elected; our parents make promises with good intentions but lack the power to keep those promises. In God, all three elements come together.

Peter uses two adjectives to describe God's promises. First, he says that they are "great". Literally, he says that God's promises are the *greatest*.[36] Later in the letter Peter uses the same word when speaking of the power of angels. But for them, he uses the form "greater" (translated "stronger" in the NIV – 2:11). The angels are greater, but God is the greatest, and so are his promises. They are in a class of their own!

We need to remember this when we are tempted to fear the anger of the ancestors or of other spirits. No spirit, not even an angel, can be greater than God. We also need to remember this when we are tempted to turn away from God by some empty human promise of success or pleasure. We need to embrace God's promises, read them, memorize them, and let them motivate and transform us. They are worth our all.

Secondly, Peter describes God's promises as precious, that is, they are of enormous value. The only other thing that the Apostle Peter describes as precious is the blood of the Lamb of God (1 Pet 1:19). This blood is closely connected to the promises, for it was through the shedding of his precious blood on the cross that all the precious promises of God are fulfilled (2 Cor 1:20). Some of these promises we have already received; some of them we do not yet have. But all of God's promises are ours and will eternally be ours in Christ Jesus. God's finished work in Christ was his final Yes to all his promises.

These promises are precious not only because they are costly – they cost Christ his life – but also because of the one who made the promise. A promise from a politician is worth nothing in comparison to any promise God makes. God is faithful, and when he promises, you can count on him. He is also so powerful that nothing and no one can prevent him from keeping his promises.

But why has God given us his promises? For the same reason that he called us. God gives us his promises so that we *may participate in the divine nature* (1:4b). He wants us to share his nature and be like him. This is not to say that we are to become "little gods", as some preachers claim. We will never have God's authority to command things to happen. Nor is God promising us wealth and health in this life. If we listen to prosperity preachers who say that he does, we are falling into the same trap we nearly did in 1:3, when we read only half the verse and assumed that the statement that Christ will give "us everything we need" referred to our getting money or a car.

The part of the divine nature that we may share is God's moral character, his holiness and moral perfection. Just as Israel was commanded, "You shall be holy, for I am holy" (Lev 11:44, 45; 19:7), so God calls us to share in his holiness (1:15–16). We are to be perfect as our heavenly Father is perfect (Matt 5:48), merciful as he is merciful (Luke 6:26), forgive as he has forgiven us (Eph 4:32; Col 3:13), walk in love as Christ loved us and gave himself for us (Eph 5:2), lay down our lives for others as Christ laid down his life for us (1 John 3:16; Phil 2:17), walk in light as he is in the light (1 John 1:7), and imitate God in the same way that children imitate their parents (Eph 5:1).

This is not something we can achieve just by mustering our willpower and relying on positive thinking. We can only share in God's divine nature if we have *escaped the corruption in the world caused by evil desires* (1:4c; see also 1 John 2:16, 17), and the only way in which we can make this escape is through Christ's power and God's promises. In fact here "escaping" is another metaphor for conversion (see also 2:18, 20).[37]

When Peter speaks of *the world* in 1:4c he is not meaning the natural universe – that we cannot escape, for we were created to live in it. The world Peter is speaking of is the God-opposing world system, as well as all our sinful desires and the things that draw us away from God. God delivers us from these – but we need to remember that we will not experience complete liberation in this life. For as long as we live, we will continue to struggle and fight sinful desires that war against our souls (see 1 Pet 2:11; Gal 5:17; 2 Tim 2:22), but through the power of Christ, we can overcome them (Gal 5:16), secure in the knowledge that complete victory will come at the end of the age (see Rom 8:23; Phil 3:20–21).

We will not totally escape corruption in this world, and we will never be perfect and flawlessly like God in this present age. We will only perfectly share in his moral excellence when we see him face to face (see 1 John 3:1–2). But this should not discourage us from pursuing these things in the present.

One way to think about this might be to see yourself as a small child, newly born into God's family. Infants need to learn to roll over, and then to crawl on their hands and knees, and then to pull themselves up on furniture before they learn to walk freely like the adults they are watching and imitating. But if a child never saw an adult walking, would that child walk? Or would he be content to crawl for the rest of his life?

In the same way, our lives are shaped by what we look at. If we focus on material things or on the power of ancestral spirits, we will not become like God. As the psalmist says, those who focus on idols become like them (Pss 115:8; 135:18). But if we focus on God's promise that one day we will be like him in moral perfection, and on Christ's power that will enable us to achieve that goal, we will grow in our knowledge of God, and as we do so, we will increasingly become like him and share in his glorious nature now.

Are you struggling with sexual temptation? Trust God's promises and keep fighting the good fight of faith, as you await the revelation of our glorious God and Saviour Jesus Christ. Meditate on the precious promises of God and be empowered to conquer the sinful tendencies in your heart.

If someone promised you one million francs or shillings this morning, it would change your entire day, but God has given you even greater promises – why not focus on them and let them have their rightful effect on your heart?

Questions for Discussion

1. How would you describe godliness in your own words?

2. How do the promises of God affect our walk with the Lord, and how are we to use them in our growth in godliness?

3. According to 2 Peter 1:3–4, God has given us everything we need for godliness. What are some of these things?

4. How do God's promises help us to share his divine nature?

5. In what specific areas of your life could you apply a particular promise of God in order to grow in holiness? Choose one promise from the Bible that is applicable to that area of struggle, memorize it, and pray it over and over until your life is affected by its transforming power.

THE POWER OF PROMISES

Peter argues that the promises of God are his gracious gifts to us to empower us and enable us to share in his divine nature. According to Peter, we become godlier by trusting God's precious promises. Reflecting on this reminds me of my relationship with my fiancée, Dominique.

In early November 2012 a mutual friend introduced me to Dominique, who later became my wife. Throughout my time of courting her, I saw the power of promises at work in very specific ways.

When I first asked Dominique whether she would let me pursue her for marriage, her response was positive, implying that she was not going to let any other man pursue her. She promised that we would pray, seek counsel, and discern what God might be doing. We promised each other that we would focus on our relationship with God and with each other, excluding any other possible suitors. Her promise had a significant effect on me in that it kept me from looking around for any other woman to court.

These promises we made before our engagement protected us from drifting and shaped the way we related to our sisters and brothers in the church. Dominique made sure that every brother around her knew she was being courted, and I did the same with our sisters. The way we interacted with these brothers and sisters changed after we had exchanged those promises.

After many prayers, counsel from our church elders, and the confirmation of believers who know us well, I asked her if she would marry me, and her response was "Yes, I will." I had been praying to hear those three words since I first made up my mind to marry Dominique. I prayed that God would be pleased to move her heart and mouth to say them, and by God's grace she spoke them to me. When she said, "Yes, I will," I gave her a ring, and we launched into serious wedding plans.

That single promise totally changed the way I have related to her since she said it. First, there has been a stronger commitment in my heart to serve her, knowing that she is going to be with me for the rest of our lives. Second, I am now acutely intentional about seeking to lead her, taking more responsibility for what happens to her than I did before her promise to me. It has become impossible for me to do anything without considering how it would benefit Dominique and strengthen our relationship with God and each other.

The promises of God are supposed to influence us in the same way and more. Just as Dominique's promise that she would marry me changed my relationship with her and even the way I live, so God's promises are intended to change the way we live.

CONFIRM YOUR CALLING

I once knew a man who claimed to be a believer in Jesus and attended a Bible-preaching church, but whose life was not even close to what one would expect of a true believer in Christ. Although he was very involved in the church he attended, he also actively participated in idol worship. He justified this by arguing that the pastor of his church is not perfect, and that he knew of pastors who secretly turned to African gods for protection. If pastors act this way, why cannot he too live a double life – claiming to be a believer in Christ as his only Saviour yet clinging so closely to idols for fear of harm? This man's lifestyle did not confirm his salvation (calling). Instead it betrayed a lack of true faith in Christ.

Are you saved? Has God called you to himself? Do you trust in Jesus alone for your salvation? I suppose all who claim some connection to Christianity would answer these questions in the affirmative. But the Apostle Peter reminds us that what matters is not just what we say but also what we do. Our answer to those questions involves not just our words but our lifestyle.

Peter has been reminding his readers of all that God in Christ has done for us. Christ has given us faith (1:1), grace, and peace (1:2), as well as all we need to enjoy eternal life and to lead godly lives (1:3a). He has called us to himself (1:3b) and given us great and precious promises (1:4). Peter leaves no room for doubt that God's work is the foundation for our Christian lives, but this does not mean that we have nothing to do. On the contrary, we need to build on the foundation that has been laid, growing in holiness by the power of God and thus confirming that we are truly saved.

1:5a The Need to Confirm Your Calling

The fact that this section begins with the words *for this reason* makes it clear that Peter is building on what he has been saying up to this point. He commands believers to act because God in Christ has acted on their behalf. We cannot hope to share in the divine nature unless we apply ourselves to pursuing moral purity, making use of all the spiritual resources that Christ has provided for us through our knowledge of God. We have to work hard at doing this, making *every effort* to progress in our faith (1:5a).[38] This phrase is repeated three times in this chapter (1:5, 10, 15), indicating how important this point is.[39]

The word translated "effort" could also mean zeal, demonstrating that the pursuit of holiness that Peter commands here is not stoic (that is, something we have to endure) or ascetic (that is, something that involves depriving ourselves of pleasure). Instead it should be a fervent, eager, and passionate pursuit – the same way a young man makes every effort to impress a young woman he admires, or an athlete makes every effort to earn a place on the national team.

We must not serve the Lord simply out of duty; it must be a delightful thing – a thing we do because it gives us joy. In the Old Testament God expected Israel not only to serve him (Deut 6:17) but to do so joyfully and gladly (Deut 28:47). The psalmist commands the congregation to serve the Lord with gladness (Ps 100:2). Paul told the Roman Christians, "Never be lacking in zeal, but keep your spiritual fervour, serving the Lord" (Rom 12:11).

I know of a man who was asked by a sorcerer to spend the night in a graveyard. He did so, hoping that the gods would see his devotion and rescue him from his problems. You may have heard of non-Christians who pray five times a day. In some cultures, people even sacrifice their children to gods. If those who serve idols, which are not gods (see 1 Cor 8:4), show such devotion in their sometimes painful obedience, how much more should we display our commitment to Christ by zealously working hard at growing in holiness.

1:5b–7 The Virtues Needed

When the Apostle Peter tells us that we need to *add to your faith*, what does he mean by faith? In this context, he is not talking about faith as a set of doctrines that we believe but about faith as loyal devotion to and dependence on Christ and his gospel. His thinking is similar to that of James, who insisted that good works must accompany true faith (Jas 2:26). If there is no sign of good works, there is also no saving faith.

Peter begins with faith because it is the foundation of all godly practices and virtue. Without faith it is impossible to please God with any other virtues (see also Heb 11:6). Peter then lists seven qualities or virtues that should characterize believers.[40]

Before we look at the list, it is important to note that these are not the only Christian virtues that believers are to seek. This is clear if we compare this list with similar lists in Romans 5:3–5 and Galatians 5:22–23 (see also 2 Cor 6:6–8; Phil 4:8–9; Col 3:12–14; 1 Tim 3:2–7; 6:11; Titus 3:1–3; Jas 3:13, 17–18; 1 Pet 3:8–9).[41]

We should also note that these virtues are not things that we should strive for in the exact sequence given here. In other words, Peter is not presenting us with a sort of "ladder" of virtues so that we have to get our feet firmly on one rung of the ladder before we can move on to the next rung. In other words, he is not saying that we have to master goodness before we can seek to master knowledge, and so on. Instead, we should be working hard to acquire all these virtues if we are to have a well-rounded Christian life.[42]

The seven virtues we are to strive to add to our faith are these:

- *Goodness* (1:5c). The faith that God has given us (1:1; Phil 1:29) must be supplemented with "goodness". The word translated "goodness" is the same word used in 1:3 to describe the moral excellence of God ("who called us by his own glory and goodness"). God is virtuous and morally excellent. Those to whom he grants faith must strive to supplement that faith with the same moral excellence. In other words, we must confess and turn away from sin and do our best to make sure that every decision and action we take is in alignment with the nature of God. This is an important part of our participation in the divine nature (1:4).

- *Knowledge* (1:5d). If we are to be like God, we need to know what God is like, and that is why believers need to strive to add knowledge to goodness. The object of this knowledge is Christ our Lord (see also 1:2, 3, 8). We must continue to grow in our knowledge of him (3:18). How do we do this? By reading and studying the Bible, which is God's word to us and testifies to Christ. When God's word fills and renews our minds, we experience transformation in our lives and in our thinking (Rom 12:2). We will then have a knowledge of God that is rooted not only in our minds but also in our experience. Such knowledge will help us to discern God's will, that is, what he wants us to do in various situations.

- *Self-control* (1:6a). Self-control is a fruit of the Holy Spirit (Gal 5:23), but that does not mean that we do not have to work hard to cultivate this fruit. With our promise-empowered ability (1:3–4), we can control our emotions, impulses, and desires and align them with God's word so that we say "yes" to godliness and "no" to sin. If we lack self-control, we will not be able to make good use of our growing knowledge of God and will repeatedly fall into sin. That is why the book of Proverbs says that someone who lacks self-control is like "a city whose walls are broken through", leaving it defenceless against its enemies (Prov 25:28 ESV). No wonder the wise King Solomon declared that someone with self-control is better "than one who takes a city" (Prov 16:32 NIV; see also Prov 14:29; 14:17, 18, 29; 15:18).

- *Perseverance* (1:6b). Self-control must be supplemented with tenacity because it is through such endurance that we will gain life (see Luke 21:19; Rom 2:7). "The need to persevere is particularly important in the situation Peter addressed, for the opponents were threatening the church, attracting others to follow them (2:2), so that some who began in the way of the gospel had since abandoned it (2:20–22)."[43] Perseverance is also required today, for we still face many trials. We should embrace this virtue with joy because by it we strengthen our characters and confirm the hope we have in Christ (Rom 5:3–5; 15:4; Jas 1:3–4).

- *Godliness* (1:6c). Godliness refers to respectful devotion to God that is reflected by purity in every area of our lives. Christ has given us all the resources we need for godliness (1:3). Because the world and all things in it will soon pass away, we must pursue godliness as a supplement to our faith in Christ (3:11).

- *Mutual affection* (1:7a). In the New Testament, the term translated "mutual affection" (or "brotherly affection" – ESV) is used only with reference to the affection that should exist between those who believe in Christ. This affection is something that the Holy Spirit stirs in our hearts (1 Thess 4:9), but it is also something that we have to work at, for we may find it difficult to love some members of our Christian family because they have difficult personalities, or a very different cultural background, or come from a group we do not like. That may be why the New Testament includes many reminders that we are to treat each other with love and respect and greet each other warmly (see, for example, 1 Pet 1:22; 5:14; Heb 13:1; Rom 12:10).

- *Love* (1:7b). Love is the supreme virtue that crowns and embraces all others (see also Col 3:4; 1 Cor 12:31–13:13).[44] It covers a multitude of sins (1 Pet 4:8). Given that Peter has already mentioned the love among believers, it is possible that what he is speaking of here is believer's love for God. If this is correct, then the last two virtues sum up the Law and the Prophets (Deut 6:5; Lev 19:18; see also Mal 4:4; Matt 22:40) as well as the teachings of Jesus (Matt 22:34–40), and Paul (Rom 13:8, 10; Gal 5:14) for the whole law is fulfilled in love for one's neighbour and love for God. (Note that while Peter focuses on love among believers, it does not follow that we are to hate unbelievers; rather, we must love those outside of Christ and seek to win them to Christ by preaching the gospel to them.)

Do you see these virtues in your life? Do you love your brothers and sisters in the faith? Give yourself to supplementing your faith with these virtues. You may want to bow and pray that God will give you the strength to forsake the sins in your life, embrace his promises, and grow in Christ-like virtues daily. After all,

> our obedience to God's commands is the expression of trusting Christ. It is not our words but our deeds that stand the test of Christ's gaze. Love of Jesus is measured by obedience to what he commands (John 14:15 and 15:14). "He who has my commandments and keeps them, he it is who loves me" (John

14:21). Not even miracles can substitute for doing what God commands (Matt 7:22).[45]

1:8–9 The Evidence Needed

Usefulness in the service of Christ is associated with our Christ-likeness, and our Christ-likeness will grow as we supplement our faith with Christian virtues. Unsupplemented faith is not only useless, it is also unproductive and yields no fruit of eternal significance. It is like a stagnant pool.

1:8 Fruitful or barren?

If we wish to be useful in Christ's service, we should be developing the good qualities listed above *in increasing measure*. If we do not do this, we will increasingly become *ineffective and unproductive* in our knowledge of Christ (1:8).

The word translated "ineffective" is the same word used in the parable of the workers in the vineyard to describe the men who were idle because they could not find work (Matt 20:3, 6). Paul also uses it when writing to Timothy about people who were idle busybodies – eager to know what everyone else was doing but too lazy to do any work of their own (1 Tim 5:13; Titus 1:12). It is also used when Jesus speaks of our being judged for our "empty words", the words we speak thoughtlessly. So someone who is ineffective in Christ's work is someone who is unproductive and, if anything, causes trouble rather than actively doing good. This is what we will be like if we do not keep growing in Christian virtues.

The word that the NIV translates as "unproductive" is actually even stronger in its meaning, as we can see from its literal translation, "unfruitful". According to the New Testament, there is no such thing as an unfruitful Christian. In the parable of the vine, Jesus makes it clear that fruitlessness indicates a lack of connection to the true vine and warns that any fruitless branches will be cut off (John 15:2–6). Paul says that the Holy Spirit produces fruit of some kind in every believer (Gal 5:22–23). So if there is no sign of any growth in virtue and no sign of any fruit of the Spirit in your life, it may be because you are not really connected to Christ.

Christ's teaching in the parable of the sower (Matt 13:8) also stresses that Christians must be fruitful. Even though some will bear more fruit than others, all true believers must produce some fruit. As James reminds us, "faith by itself, if it is not accompanied by action, is dead" (Jas 2:17). By contrast, a faith that is effective and productive is clear evidence that one is truly a child of God, or in other words, that your calling and election are sure (1:10). Knowledge of Christ created in the crucible of experience will inevitably be seen to be "bearing fruit in every good work" (Col 1:10).

It is very common in Africa for people to base their faith on a miracle that some "prophet" or prosperity preacher performed for them. Such faith is not true faith. True faith is rooted in Christ's death and resurrection, not in miracles, wealth, or good health, and it is evidenced by an ever-growing longing for godliness and conformity to Christ.

Are you growing in godliness or you are only growing in your desire for more miracles? You must have good works in keeping with repentance and not presume on your religious pedigree for your standing before God (Matt 3:8–10).

1:9 Sighted or blind?

So-called believers who lack the Christian virtues are not only "ineffective and unproductive", they are also *near-sighted and blind*.[46] Here Peter is not speaking about physical blindness but about the spiritual blindness or near-sightedness that prevents these people from looking back and seeing what Christ has done for them. They are oblivious to his grace displayed on the cross of Calvary.

In the Old Testament, blindness is often used as a metaphor for spiritual deadness and divine judgement (see Gen 19:11; Deut 28:28; 2 Kgs 6:18; Zech 12:4; Job 5:14; 12:25; Isa 59:10; Zeph 1:17). In the New Testament, we read of some who were physically blind, but there were far more who were spiritually blind and failed to see the glory of God in the face of Christ. Jesus often accused the Pharisees of being blind (Matt 15:14; 23:16–19, 24–26; Rom 2:19). God has judged the world so that those who claim to see – the Pharisees and others – may not see, whereas those who confess their spiritual blindness do see (John 9:39–41).

The Holy Spirit was given to give sight to the blind (Luke 4:18). One sign that he is at work is that those who were once spiritually blind, and thus unloving, now love their brothers and sisters (1 John 2:9–11) and remember with gratitude what Christ has done for them. By contrast, those who are blind have forgotten *that they have been cleansed from their past sins* (1:9).

Cleansing or purification is another important theme in the Old Testament. Large sections of the book of Leviticus deal with the purification of people and objects. When Peter speaks of people having "been cleansed", he is not thinking of those old rituals but of the New Testament ritual of water baptism, which symbolizes spiritual cleansing from sin (Acts 2:38; 22:16). When believers remember their baptism, they remember that God has washed away all their guilt. To forget something that momentous is equivalent to wilful blindness. Those who indulge in this blindness will also be blind to the virtues listed in 1:5–7. They are acting like a married person who throws away his or her wedding ring, ignores the marriage covenant and their commitment to their spouse, and pretends to be single again. This course of action often leads to adultery, which dishonours both God and their spouse.

In the Old Testament forgetting the past redeeming work of Yahweh was a mark of spiritual depravity because it inevitably led to the worship of other gods (see Deut 4:23; 8:19), disobedience to Yahweh (Deut 6:12; 8:11, 14), and judgement (Deut 8:19). Similarly, if believers in Christ forget about the forgiveness of their sins signified by water baptism, they will inevitably start to neglect the life of holiness, which is evidence that their hearts are not truly right with God.

How do we guard against developing spiritual "cataracts" and slipping into blindness ourselves? By reading the Bible often to remind ourselves of all that God has done for us in Christ Jesus, fellowshipping with other believers, praying for God to guard our faith, and striving towards holiness daily. If we are in Christ, God has saved us, washed us from all our sins, justified us, and adopted us into his family! We should respond with gratitude and obedience.

1:10–11 The Need to Confirm One's Calling

Given how crucial it is to possess and be increasing in the Christ-like virtues listed in 1:5–7, Peter concludes (as shown by the *therefore*) that believers must practise those virtues in order to guard themselves against apostasy and ensure that they are warmly welcomed into Christ's kingdom. He exhorts us as his *brothers and sisters* in Christ (see also Matt 12:50; Rom 8:29) to *make every effort to confirm your calling and election* (1:10). The Greek word translated "confirm" or "make . . . sure" (KJV) implies validating something.[47] Think about what happens when you buy more minutes for your mobile phone. You have paid for those minutes, but you cannot use them until you enter the validating code on your phone. That code validates your right to use those minutes. Similarly, we have already been bought by the blood of Christ, but our godly living is like the validating code on our calling and election. If you throw away the receipt before entering the validating code, you can never use the minutes you paid for. And if you do not bother to acquire the virtues that should accompany faith in Christ, your faith may not be genuine. There are also some who fraudulently claim to have bought minutes when they did not. Their lack of a validating code proves that their claim is false. In the same way, there are those who claim to be saved, but are not. The proof that they are unsaved is that there is no sign at all that they are pursuing godliness.

When Peter speaks of our *calling* he is not referring to our vocation, which is how this word is often used in everyday speech. Rather, he is referring to the effective work of God in our hearts to draw us to Christ. The calling is God's call to come to Christ. Our *election* too has nothing to do with everyday politics but refers to God's sovereign choice of us for salvation before the foundation of the world (Eph 1:4; 1 Pet 2:9). Calvin rightly argues that this command to confirm our calling means, "Labour that you may have it really proved that you have not been called . . . in vain."[48]

Believers confirm God's calling and election by practising the virtues that Peter lists in 1:5–7. If we claim that we are of the elect and the called, we must prove it by our pursuit of holiness. We are right to question the calling of people like the false teachers mentioned in chapter 2 whose life shows no evidence of godliness.

Peter also assures his readers that those who pursue godliness *will never stumble* (1:10b).[49] This point is made very strongly in the Greek, highlighting the fact that they will never ever fall away from the faith.[50] If we practise the Christ-like virtues in 1:5–7, we can be sure of our calling and election and can have an immovable and invincible assurance that we will never stumble and fall to destruction.

This does not mean that we will never sin. We will not achieve sinless perfection this side of eternity. But we can be confident that we will not be like marathon runners who lack stamina and drop out half way through the race; we will reach the finish line in our race of faith and will be welcomed into the kingdom of Christ.[51]

Not only will we be welcomed, we will receive *a rich welcome* (1:11a) – the superabundant reward that God will give to all believers. This is what we will *receive,* for it is what God will provide. If we supplement our faith with godly virtues, we will receive a sumptuous welcome at the end of the age. This is not salvation by works but, as Schreiner rightly notes: "it is salvation *with* works."[52]

The terms "kingdom of God" or "kingdom of Christ" do not appear in the Old Testament, although God is clearly presented as reigning over creation (Gen 14:19, 22; 2 Kgs 19:15; Isa 37:16). In the book of Psalms he is celebrated as king over all creation (Pss 93:1; 96:4–10; 104; 136). But the New Testament contains many references to the kingdom of God (Matt 19:24; Mark 10:15; Luke 18:17; John 3:5; Acts 14:22; Rom 14:17).

When Peter talks of *the eternal kingdom of our Lord and Saviour Jesus Christ* (1:11b; see also Col 1:13), he does not mean that there are two separate kingdoms, that is, a kingdom of God and a separate kingdom of Jesus. No, Jesus rules the same kingdom as his Father (see Eph 5:5). Christ now reigns, and he will hand over the kingdom to the Father after destroying all his enemies (1 Cor 15:24). Then he will reign with his Father, forever (Rev 3:21; 11:15), in the company of those who have not rejected his present reign (Luke 19:27; 2 Tim 2:12; Rev 3:21; 20:6).

Does he reign now over you, over your marriage or your singleness, your work and your leisure? If he is not reigning over you now, you shall not reign with him.

Questions for Discussion

1. Is it significant that Peter uses the first person plural pronoun "us" in 1:3, 4 and the second person plural pronoun "you" in 1:5, 8, 10, 12, 13, 15 (as well as a second person plural verb in the Greek of 1:4, 5, 10) in talking about what God has done, and what he expects of us to confirm his work for us? Does that suggest that growth in holiness is a community affair? If yes, how can we grow together as a community in godliness based on Peter's teaching in 1:1–11?

2. In what practical ways can we daily make our election sure? How can we be sure that we are supplementing our faith with all the virtues listed in 1:5–7? Is it possible to have some of those things and not have true faith?

REMEMBER THE APOSTOLIC PREACHING

Centuries before Peter's time, King Solomon wrote, "My son, do not forget my teaching, but keep my commands in your heart . . . do not let wisdom and understanding out of your sight" (Prov 3:1, 21). Those words would have resonated with the Apostle Peter as he wrote out his final instructions to his spiritual children. He had already taught them the truth about Christ, but he wanted to remind them how important his teaching was for their future well-being. They must not forget it after he is gone.

So Peter reminds his readers of things they already know (1:12–15) and shares his experiences with them (1:16–21). He reminds them that the words of the apostles and prophets are completely trustworthy and should be held on to, even though they are being challenged by false teachers. The truths they have been taught by Peter and his fellow apostles provide what they need to please God as they stand on God's work of grace (1:3–4).

1:12–15 The Need to be Reminded

Sometimes we become bored when our parents or teachers tell us the same things over and over again. We think, "I already know that." But rather than dismissing what they are saying, we should recognize that there is a reason for the repetitions: the things they are repeating are extremely important and our elders know the dangers we will face if we forget the truths they are communicating. Similarly, Peter is speaking like a parent when he brings up the theme of remembrance three times in four verses, saying, *I will always remind you of these things* (1:12a); *I think it is right to refresh your memory* (1:13), and *I will make every effort to see that . . . you will always be able to remember these things* (1:15).

What is it that Peter wants his readers to remember? What does he mean by "these things"? He is referring to everything he has been saying up to this point about God's grace and the need to continue to grow in godliness and be fruitful in order to confirm that we are true believers.

Peter uses the future tense, "I will" when he talks about reminding them not only because this is what he would like to do until he draws his last breath but also because he hopes that his letter will have an enduring effect on the church, even after his own death.[53] His hopes have been fulfilled – two thousand years later, we are still reading his words.

Very few of us would forget or ignore the words of a dying parent or grandparent. Surely we should take even more seriously the words of the dying apostle, which bring God's message to us. We should read them, memorize them, pray them, study them, and live them.

The fact that the apostle's ministry outlived him should also fill writers, teachers, and preachers with both joy and fear: Joy because your ministry will outlast you and may yield more fruit than you ever imagined, and fear because if you write, preach, or teach what is false, you will keep propagating heresy to future generations who will read or listen to your works. Preachers must uphold nothing but the truth because the effects of their sermons may be more far-reaching than they ever imagined.

It is worth noting that Peter says that even those who know the apostolic teaching so well that they are *firmly established in the truth*[54] still benefit from reminders (1:12b). Every believer, including those who have been believers for many years, needs regular reminders about all that the apostles taught about God and what God has done for us. Those who know the truth must be reminded of the truth.

One reason why such reminders are needed is embedded in Peter's use of the word *refresh* in 1:13a, where he speaks about refreshing their memories. The word he uses occurs only five times in the New Testament and of those five, three are found in the story of Jesus' calming of the storm. You will remember that Jesus was asleep in the boat as he and the disciples were crossing the lake. When a sudden storm struck, the terrified disciples woke Jesus from sleep (Mark 4:38; Luke 8:24). The verb translated "woke" in that context is the same one translated "refresh" (or "stir you up", ESV) in 2 Peter. We can conclude that by reminding believers of the truth, we are stirring them up so that they do not spiritually fall asleep (see also 3:1). In fact, those who are lulling themselves into spiritual slumber are often charged to rise: "So then, let us not be like others, who are asleep, but let us be awake and sober" (1 Thess 5:6; see also Joel 1:5; Eph 5:14).

Peter, aware of the brevity of life, speaks of his body as being no more than a *tent* (1:13b). This is a powerful image of mortality (see also 2 Cor 5:1, 4). A tent is not a permanent structure but a temporary home of the type the patriarchs lived in (Heb 11:9–10). The Israelites too had lived in tents while travelling through the wilderness on their way to the promised land.

As one who has a deep burden and calling from the Lord to feed and shepherd God's flock (John 21:15–19; 1 Pet 5:1–4), Peter takes every opportunity to do so while he is still alive, or still "in his tent". In this he is like Moses, another leader who was well aware that the time of his death was near (Deut 4:22; 31:14; 34:5). Like Peter, he used his final days to urge those he led to remember the words and deeds of Yahweh (Deut 8:2; 11:18). We as pastors and spiritual leaders must make the best use of our brief God-given time (Eph 5:15). We do not know the time of our passing from this life, but the knowledge that we all still live in "tents" should affect the way we live and serve God.

Peter did his utmost to remind the believers of the truths they had been taught (1:15). He urged them to do their utmost to live out their calling as disciples. Now it is our turn to do our utmost to remember the words of the apostle by reading what he has written, mediating on it, and applying these truths to our own lives.

1:16–18 Remember the Incarnate Word

The advice parents give to their children is often rooted in their own experience. The same is true of the teaching of the apostles. They spoke and wrote authoritatively because they attested to historical events that they themselves had witnessed. Peter himself had heard Christ speak, had seen Christ's power at work, had seen his glory and heard the majestic voice of the Father. So Peter is utterly convinced that what he and the other apostles (*we*) have been proclaiming is factual and not a *cleverly devised story* (1:16a). This is another reason why he will not stop reminding his readers about it.[55]

Parents on their deathbeds do not waste their time telling their children made-up stories. They know their time is short, and what they need to communicate is what will most affect their children's futures. In the same way, Peter is concerned only to communicate what is true. Like the Apostle Paul, he rejects "stories" or "myths" because they cannot advance godliness (1 Tim 1:4; 4:7; 2 Tim 4:4; Titus 1:14), uphold the power of the cross (1 Cor 1:17), or advance God's work (1 Tim 1:4). Our faith should not be rooted in human ingenuity but in the power of God (1 Cor 2:4–5).

This is a point we still need to remember. There are many who are willing to tell stories and even give testimonies today that have little relationship to what actually happened (a fact that is sometimes even reported in newspapers, to our shame). We need to remember that just because a testimony is fascinating does not mean that it is factual. Those of us who are pastors have a particular responsibility to preach the gospel in truth, and not waste our time and that of our listeners on wild stories and idle speculations (1 Tim 4:7).

Peter summarizes what he and his fellow apostles ("we") proclaimed as *the coming of our Lord Jesus Christ in power* (1:16b). Here the *coming* referred to is not Jesus' first coming to earth but his second coming (Matt 24:3; 1 Cor 15:23; 1 Thess 3:13; 2 Thess 2:1, 8), which false teachers were questioning (1 Pet 3:4).[56] The apostles proclaimed that he would be returning in "power", displaying his sovereign authority over all things (Matt 28:18; Phil 2:9).

While this coming has not happened yet, Peter and his fellow apostles know that it will come because they have already been *eyewitnesses of his majesty* (1:16c). The word translated *majesty* is the same one used with reference to the mighty power of God in Luke 9:43, which suggests that here too Peter implies the divinity of Christ.

The apostles were first-hand witnesses to the historical divine Messiah, and their teaching is rooted in that history (see also John 19:35; 1 John

1:1). Preachers today do not have the same kind of exposure to Christ as they did, but will be better preachers if they preach biblical truths that have affected them personally – truths that have transformed them. Excellent preachers are formed in the crucible of their God-centred and biblically informed experience of Christ's majesty.

In 1:17–18 Peter recounts the event that most displayed Christ's majesty, the transfiguration. What took place on the Mount of Transfiguration is what is technically called a theophany (Matt 17:1; Mark 9:2; Luke 9:28–29). The same term is used of God's appearances to Moses and Elijah (Exod 19, 20, 34; 1 Kgs 19:8–34).

One fascinating detail of the gospel account of the transfiguration is the topic of the conversation between the majestic Christ and Moses and Elijah, who also appeared on the mountain. In Luke's account, Moses and Elijah spoke with Jesus about his "exodus" (departure) (Luke 9:31). This departure was Christ's death, yet the word chosen to refer to it alludes to the redemptive work of God in the exodus, when he brought the Israelite slaves out of Egypt to create a people for himself. It is as if Luke wants us to see that Jesus accomplishes a new exodus through his death to create a new people for God. The Father honoured and glorified his Son for the redemptive work he was about to accomplish.

It is striking that it is God the Father who gives the son *honour and glory* (1:17a), for in both the Old Testament and the New, honour and glory are ascribed to the Father (Ps 29:1; 96:7; 1 Tim 1:17; Rev 4:11; 7:12). In the New Testament, however, these qualities are also ascribed to the Son (Heb 2:9; Rev 5:12–13), signifying that the Father and the Son share glory and honour. In fact the New Testament shows that there is mutual glorification within the Godhead, with each honouring the other. Jesus glorified the Father (John 17:4), and the Father glorified Jesus (John 17:1; 2 Peter 1:17).

Peter witnessed the Father honouring the majestic Son on the Mount of Transfiguration when he heard the majestic voice saying, *This is my Son, whom I love; with him I am well pleased* (1:17b). These words are similar to the Father's words to the Son at the time of his baptism, an action that prefigured the Son's suffering under God's wrath at the cross (Matt 3:17; Mark 1:11; Luke 3:22). The Father honoured the Son for his willingness to drink the cup of God's judgement on behalf of others (see Phil 2:8–11).[57]

When Jesus was transfigured, his face was altered so that it shone like the sun (Luke 9:29a; Matt 17:2). His clothes became intensely white, whiter than any bleach on earth could make them (Mark 9:3; Luke 9:29b). This description of Christ is similar to the revelation that was given to John on the island of Patmos, where he saw the resurrected Christ whose "face was like the sun shining in full strength" (Rev 1:16 ESV). The sight would have recalled Daniel's vision of the Ancient of Days: "As I looked, thrones were placed, and the Ancient of Days took his seat; his clothing was white as snow" (Dan 7:9 ESV; see also Rev 1:14; 20:4). At the transfiguration, Jesus was unveiled to the disciples as the figure in this vision.

Jesus did not allow the disciples to talk about what they had seen on the mountain, until after his resurrection (Matt 17:9; Mark 9:9). So they had kept silent about their awe-inspiring experience (Luke 9:36). Now, however, Peter can freely write to believers about the event and give it as a reason for them to accept what he and the other apostles have taught them. Peter writes as one who has heard God and seen Jesus' majestic glory. Having received a glimpse of the glorified Christ, Peter and the apostles proclaim his future coming (*parousia*).

The experience of the apostles validates their words. After Moses descended from Mount Sinai with his face shining because he had been in God's presence, he brought the law of God to Israel and expected them to receive it as the word of the Lord. Likewise, Peter expects the church to receive the prophetic word of the apostles because they have seen the majesty of Christ at the transfiguration, have heard the majestic voice of the Father, and have been commissioned by the resurrected Christ to proclaim his majesty.

1:19–21 Remember the Inspired Word

The Apostle Peter has been saying that his words deserve to be remembered because he is not making things up but is reporting on something he knows from experience. That, however, is not the only reason his readers must pay close attention to remembering what they have been taught. Another reason is that Peter and the other apostles *also have the prophetic message as something completely reliable* (1:19a).[58]

The prophets' words were also not "cleverly devised stories" and did not originate in human imagination.

The *prophetic message* could be more literally translated as "the prophetic word" (ESV, NASB),[59] an expression that was used to refer to the Old Testament Scriptures (see Rom 16:26).[60] The apostles do not have to rely solely on experience, but have something that is even more reliable, God's prophetic word.[61] This is what confirms the truth of their experience. This point emerges even more clearly if we look at the KJV translation of this chapter, which reflects the Greek words used: "make your calling and election sure" (1:10) and "a more sure word of prophecy" (1:19). Just as our actions confirm our calling, so the prophetic word confirms the apostles' experience. Scripture is more certain than events and experience and must be used to evaluate experience.

The prophetic word, Peter says, is like *a light shining in a dark place* (1:19). This imagery finds its roots in the Old Testament: "Your word is a lamp to my feet and a light on my path" (Ps 119:105). This light of the prophetic word illuminates the path of the righteous, and it shines brighter and brighter until the full day (Prov 4:18). Just as light dispels darkness, so the prophetic word dissipates the darkness of false teachings. So if your church is plagued with false teaching, keep teaching the word of God because the darkness of erroneous teaching cannot stand the life-giving light of God's word. The word of God created light out of darkness (Gen 1:2–3), and can also shed light in hearts that have been confused by false teaching and darkened by sin (2 Cor 4:6).

Believers must rely on the prophetic word *until the day dawns and the morning star rises in your hearts* (1:19b; see also Rom 13:12). The dawning of the day means the coming of the time of final judgement and salvation, and the morning star figuratively refers to Christ. The Old Testament speaks of the coming day of the Lord as a day when the Lord would judge the wicked (Isa 13:6, 9; Jer 46:10). Amos described it as a day of darkness (Amos 5:18–20). Believers, however, will welcome that day when the Lord returns to save his people and Christ, *the morning star*, appears to light their way.

Revelation 22:16 identifies Christ as "the bright Morning Star", confirming our connection of the rising of the morning star to Christ's return. This image has its roots in Balaam's prophecy that "a star will come out of Jacob; a sceptre will rise out of Israel" and will destroy the enemies of God's people (Num 24:17). Since Jesus is the Morning Star, we can construe the phrase "until . . . the morning star rises in our hearts" to mean that when Jesus returns, he will be our light in place of the prophetic word, which now shines as light in a dark place.[62] The prophetic word, like a lamp, will be eclipsed in the blazing sun of the Son of God at his second coming.

Peter states two reasons why his audience must pay attention to the prophetic word. First, negatively, he argues, *no prophecy of Scripture came about by the prophet's own interpretation of things* (1:20b). The verse begins, *above all, you must understand*. For Peter, it is of primary importance that we know that the words of prophecy were never human ideas; the prophets spoke God's infallible word. Thus, we must receive the word of Scripture as the word of God (1 Thess 2:13).

This reminder is very important in this age when many question the authority of Scripture and actively undermine it. The church in Africa, for example, is full of prophets who claim to speak for God but actually speak their own ideas. They never challenge people to live godly lives, but instead make fake promises that are not rooted in the reliable word of Scripture but in the preacher's own desire to become wealthy. They promise people wealth and good health if they "sow seeds" to the preachers. The fact that we never see any true prophets doing such things in Scripture makes it clear that such preachers are crafting things from their own minds and for selfish ends, seeking to enrich themselves and feeding on the flock instead of feeding the flock. But according to 1:21a, true *prophecy never had its origin in the human will*. False prophets speak their own desires and will (Jer 23:16–17), but true prophets speak God's word for God's people.

Second, positively, Peter argues that true prophets, *though human, spoke from God as they were carried along by the Holy Spirit* (1:21b). When we study the Scripture, we must keep in mind that the prophets did not make up what they spoke by themselves. God called the prophets (Amos 2:11) and God spoke by his Spirit through them (2 Sam 23:2; Neh 9:30; Acts 3:18). The Spirit of God was in the true prophets (Neh 9:30; 2 Sam 23:2; see also 1 Pet 1:10–11) and moved them to speak his word (Heb 1:1). This reminder is important for us as we read Peter's letter, for it and the rest of the Scriptures were inspired by the Holy Spirit.

Those of us who preach the gospel must take care not to base our sermons on human stories, even if they are true stories. These stories may sometimes be used to illustrate a point, but they should not be at the core of our preaching (see 1 Cor 4:6). Rather, our preaching must be based on the infallible word of God.

Questions for Discussion

1. Why was it important for Peter to point out that the Holy Spirit inspired the prophets and that they did not speak on their own account? How should this change our approach to and use of the Scriptures, both the Old and New Testaments?

2. Consider this true story. A preacher claimed to have words of prophecy for the church every Sunday morning. When another preacher challenged him that what he was doing was wrong and contrary to Scriptures, this preacher said it was okay to make up things and proclaim them. He argued that it did not matter whether his prophecies were fulfilled or not because they met needs at the time he spoke them. He argued that preachers need to go beyond the written word and "operate in the realm of the Spirit".

   How would you respond to such a preacher who thinks that it is not important to preach the Scriptures, but simply to follow "the leading of the Spirit?"

3. Does the New Testament have the same authority as the Old Testament? Consider 1 Thessalonians 2:13; 1 Peter 1:10–11 and 2 Peter 3:14–16 in discussing this question.

4. List five possible ways that Peter's instructions to the church in this section can be applied to present-day preachers and teachers. What would Peter say to the church today concerning attentiveness to God's word?

5. What steps can you take to ensure that you and those you lead remember the words of God?

BEWARE OF FALSE TEACHERS

A story is told about a businessman who borrowed a horse from his neighbour. While it was in his possession, the horse died. Naturally, the owner was upset and insisted on being paid the value of the horse, with some compensation for the loss of its use. The businessman agreed to pay, but said that he did not have the cash on hand. So he offered to write a promissory note, a binding promise that he would hand over the money by a certain date. The owner agreed to this arrangement and allowed the businessman to set the date on which the money would be due. This was a mistake. When he looked at the promissory note the businessman had given him, he found that payment would only be due at the judgement day.

The owner of the horse was angry and took the matter to court. There the businessman argued that his promissory note was legal because the other man had accepted it, and so he did not need to pay for the horse yet.

The judge agreed with him that the promissory note was legally binding. But the businessman's rejoicing at getting away with cheating his neighbour faded at the judge's next words: "However, today is judgement day in this court, and so I decree that you must pay the debt now."[63]

For this man, the judgement day came at a time he did not expect, and he was found guilty. Peter makes a similar point about the false teachers. They too think they can get away with lies and deceit, but they will face

God's judgement. This is a point we need to remember, for there are still false preachers in Africa. If we share Peter's longing for people to grow in grace and the knowledge of God (1:2; 2:20; 3:18), we need to warn them against false teachers who will stunt their growth and lead them far away from God.

2:1a The Presence of False Teachers

Just as there are honest businessmen and corrupt businessmen, so there are honest prophets and false prophets, true teachers and false teachers. In the previous section of this letter, Peter argued that he and his fellow apostles could be trusted because they were eyewitnesses of Jesus' life and work. The church should therefore pay attention to their teaching, which contains not their own opinions but truths revealed to them by Christ and the Holy Spirit. Peter contrasts the apostles who are true prophets with false prophets, introducing the contrast with the word *but*, and showing that not everyone who claims to be a prophet is true.

The presence of false prophets is nothing new – they were present *among the people*, that is, among God's covenant people,[64] in the Old Testament (2:1a; see Deut 13:1–6; 1 Kgs 13:18; 18:19–22; 22:6–25; Jer 23:16–17)[65] and so can be expected to be present *among you*, that is, among God's new covenant people, the church. History does repeat itself.

Moreover, Jesus had warned his disciples about false prophets when he told them the parable of the weeds (Matt 13:24–30). If we want to put this in contemporary terms, we could say that these teachers are like the HIV virus, which enters the body and disguises itself so that our immune system does not recognize it. Then it infects cell after cell, until the person develops full-blown AIDS, which destroys them. That is exactly how the false teachers work in the church, and that explains Peter's strong language when he speaks of them. It also explains why we need to be on guard against false teachers in our own day. Like the doctors, nurses and other educators who teach people how to avoid infection with HIV, pastors must warn Christians so that they do not become infected with false teaching.

2:1b–3a The Characteristics of False Teachers

Peter mentions five characteristics of the false teachers in his day. Sadly, we can still recognize these traits in preachers today.

2:1b They secretly introduce destructive heresies

Any teaching that is contrary to the prophetic message and the apostle's teaching, or in other words, contrary to true Christian beliefs, is heresy (see 1:19–21). Prophets are supposed to speak for God, bringing his word to his people and leading them to eternal life, but false prophets bring a false message and lead people away from saving truth and into danger. Their teaching is therefore *destructive*, a word that is frequently used in the New Testament in the context of eternal destruction (see Matt 7:13; John 17:12; Rom 9:22; Phil 1:28; 3:19; Heb 10:39). True teaching brings eternal life (John 6:68; Phil 2:16), but heresy destroys forever. That is why the Apostle Paul goes so far as to describe heresy as "things taught by demons" (1 Tim 4:1).

Because the false prophets operate *secretly*, it can be difficult to identify them at first, for they look very similar to true teachers. Paul describes them as "masquerading as apostles of Christ" (2 Cor 11:13). They are like spies, wearing a disguise as they infiltrate the church (Gal 2:4). Jesus used a vivid metaphor when he warned his followers to "beware of false prophets, who come to you in sheep's clothing but inwardly are ravenous wolves" (Matt 7:15 NRSV; see also Acts 20:29–31).

We must thus not be gullible and believe every teacher we hear. Like the Berean Christians, we need to check what our teachers say against the whole of God's word in order to know whether what they are teaching is true or false (Acts 17:13)

2:1c They deny the sovereign Lord who bought them

The Greek word translated *sovereign Lord* is used elsewhere in the context of the relationship between a servant or slave and the master (or lord) of a household (1 Tim 6:1, 2; 2 Tim 2:21; Titus 2:9; 1 Pet 2:18). It is also used when addressing God the Father in prayer (Luke 2:29; Acts 4:24; Rev 6:10). Here, however, and in Jude 4, it is used to refer to Jesus, who is the one who *bought* people for God (see also Rev 5:9; 1 Cor 6:20; 7:23), whom the false teachers are rejecting.

Peter's words raise a problem for us. If these false teachers were "bought" by Christ, does that mean that they are actually followers of Christ? No – Peter is talking about false prophets who are acting as though they are true believers, even going so far as to share in the Lord's Supper (2:13). But while outwardly they pretend to follow Christ, inwardly they deny him. There are several pointers to the fact that they cannot be true believers:

1. They deny Jesus (2:1). No true believers would do this (1 John 2:18–23; 4:3). Those who deny Christ are unbelievers and Christ will deny them when he comes again (Matt 10:33).

2. They are destined for destruction and "their condemnation has long been hanging over them" (2:3). Those whose condemnation is predetermined cannot have been bought effectively by the death of Jesus. God knows how to rescue those who are his own (2:9).

3. They are "slaves of depravity" (2:19). True believers, although they were once slaves to sin (Rom 6:16, 17), are now slaves to righteousness (Rom 6:18, 19) and to God (Rom 6:22).

4. They have some knowledge of Christ but have become entangled in and overcome by the corruption of the world (2:20). True believers do not allow themselves to become entangled in sin. Although they may sometimes fall into sin, they are not conquered by it because they rise each time they fall (2 Tim 2:4; see also Prov 24:16; Ps 37:24; Mic 7:8–10).

Thus we can say that these people deny Jesus because they are not and never were his own. They simply act as though they have been bought by Christ's blood.

2:2a They encourage depraved conduct

These teachers encourage *depraved conduct* or "sensuality" (ESV, NASB), that is, self-indulgent conduct that goes against the norms of the Christian community. The same Greek word is often used in the New Testament to refer to sexual sin (Rom 13:13; 2 Cor 12:21; Gal 5:19; Eph 4:19). That may be the meaning here, for the broader context shows that these teachers were indulging in sexual sin (see 2:7, 10, 12–14; 3:3).[66] The lifestyle they teach goes directly against the grain of the Christian virtues listed in 1:5–7. Unfortunately, such teaching is always popular, and there are many within the church who follow those who encourage it and are led astray (see Acts 20:30; Matt 24:11).

2:2b They bring the way of truth into disrepute

The *way of truth* is the way of Christ, the gospel way, which is also called "the right way" (2:15), "the way of righteousness" (2:21), "the way of the Lord" (Acts 18:25), and "the way of God" (Acts 18:26). The behaviour of false teachers gives the gospel a bad name, and makes it look far less than truth.

This is something we need to be aware of as we engage in evangelism today. If we live in obedience to the gospel and the word of God, others will be attracted to Christ. But if we are hypocrites, leading immoral lives, misappropriating church funds, abusing our positions, or neglecting our families, neither we nor our message will be respected. People will turn away from the gospel because of our behaviour (see also Titus 2:5; 1 Tim 6:1; Rom 2:24). The same thing will happen if we tolerate false teachers, for outsiders will assume that we are in agreement with those who indulge in shameful behaviour.

2:3a They are motivated by greed

Greed refers to an insatiable craving for more than one needs. Paul sees *greed* as equivalent to idolatry (Col 3:5). Someone who is greedy is motivated more by what they want for themselves than by their desire to serve God. The false teachers about whom Peter writes can even be called "experts in greed" (2:14). They are professional confidence tricksters, with so little concern for the truth of what they preach that they will happily make up stories. They see preaching as a way to make money. In fact, the Greek word translated *exploit* could be used to refer to a business transaction, as it is in James 4:13, which talks about people discussing business plans.[67] For the false teachers, ministry has become a business aimed at satisfying their covetousness. Their behaviour reminds us of the cynical saying, "If you want to get rich, start a church".

The successors of these false teachers are still at large. A Kenyan preacher who drew thousands to his church by claiming to perform miracles was exposed by the media as a charlatan who expected to be paid before he would pray for someone, staged fake healings, and encouraged fake testimonies. He is not the only preacher in Africa to operate like this. Such pastors are predators who exploit their followers by inviting them to give money in order to receive healing and other blessings. When their trickery is exposed, those who are opposed to the church rejoice while others turn away from the gospel.

What a contrast between such preachers and the apostles, who did not take advantage of anyone but made themselves poor so that others could be rich with the gospel of Christ (2 Cor 6:10). What a contrast between such preachers and Christ himself, who "though he was rich, yet for your sake he became poor, so that you through his poverty might become rich" (2 Cor 8:9; see also Phil 2:6–8). Jesus was not driven by a desire to gain something from the church but by his desire to honour God by laying down his life for the church (John 15:13). We are called to imitate him and lay down our lives for others, giving away our possessions rather than hoarding them (1 John 3:16–18).

Paul writes as a true pastor when he says,

> The appeal we make does not spring from error or impure motives, nor are we trying to trick you. On the contrary, we speak as those approved by God to be entrusted with the gospel. We are not trying to please people but God, who tests our hearts. (1 Thess 2:3–4)

2:3b–10a The Fate of False Teachers

The false teachers do not honour God, and they question Christ's second coming because of its delay (3:4–5), but their own fate will not be delayed. Their success will be short-lived, and then will come sudden destruction (2:1). Peter is not alone in saying that false teachers will be destroyed. The same fate is predicted for them by the Apostle Paul (2 Cor 11:15; 2 Thess 1:9; Phil 1:28; 3:18–19) and other New Testament writers (Matt 7:22–23; Rev 19:20; 20:10).

Peter personifies the coming destruction of the false teachers when he says that *their destruction has not been sleeping* (2:3b). Our minds immediately turn to the one whom the psalmist told us "will neither slumber or sleep" (Ps 121:4). God is the judge who will order their destruction, and he never sleeps. False gods may do this (see Elijah's taunts of the Baal worshippers in 1 Kgs 18:27), but the God of Israel is always awake and alert, and he knows what the false prophets are doing. When he acts in judgement, those he uses as the instruments of his judgement do not slumber either (Isa 5:27).

At times, of course, from our perspective it may seem that God's judgement is sleeping because he does not act as quickly as we want him to (see, for example, Pss 3:7; 7:6; 9:19; 44:23). In fact those who act wickedly prefer to assume that he is sleeping (3:3–4, 8–9).[68] But he will soon rise to condemn the wicked and save the righteous (see Pss 12:5; 35:23; 59:4–5; 73:20; 78:65; Isa 51:9).

To explain why he is so confident that God will act, Peter gives three examples of God's judgements in the past. In reminding his hearers of these stories, Peter is acting like some African traditional leaders who tell traditional stories about how the ancestors have supposedly punished those who failed to honour them. The goal of such stories is to make people conform to traditions out of fear of provoking the ancestors to anger and incurring their wrath.

Similarly but positively, Peter intends the story of God's judgements in history to instil fear and obedience. So he reminds his readers of God's judgement on angels (2:4), the ancient world (2:5), and Sodom and Gomorrah (2:6).[69] He strings all these examples together in one long sentence made up of three conditional clauses and a main clause. The conditional clauses are introduced by *if* and describe God's actions in the past, while the main clause (verse 9) draws a conclusion from those actions.[70] The whole section can be summed up by saying that God's past judgement foreshadows his future judgement on the wicked. We can be certain that he will judge them.

2:4–8 Three examples of the fate of false teachers

All the examples of God's judgement that Peter refers to come from the book of Genesis, a book that Jewish Christians would have known well, and would have taught to their non-Jewish fellow believers.

2:4 Example 1: The condemnation of angels

The first example is that God punished even *angels when they sinned* (2:4). Peter does not tell us what sin the angels committed, but he is most likely refering to the mysterious incident referred to in Genesis 6:1–4 in which the "sons of God" had sexual relations with the daughters of men, resulting in giant offspring.[71] The exact identification of what happened is less important than the point that even powerful angelic beings are not immune to eternal judgement. God consigned them to "chains of darkness" (2:4, 17; Jude 6, 13), where they await the final judgement (2:4, 9, 11; 3:7).[72] In like manner, the fate of false teachers is certain, even though their judgement is delayed. If even angels could not escape divine judgement, how can any predatory preacher or false prophet or fake healer hope to do so?

2:5 Example 2: The condemnation of the ancient world

Genesis 6:1–4 tells of the increasing wickedness in the time leading up to the great flood that brought judgement at a global level. God had commanded humans to multiply (Gen 1:28), but it was evil that was multiplying and he was grieved (Gen 6:5–6). Eventually he decided to "wipe from the face of the earth the human race I have created" (Gen 6:7).[73]

There was, however, one exception to this universal judgement. God decided to save one person, Noah (Gen 6:8). Peter's refers to him as *a preacher of righteousness* (2:5), although Noah is not called a preacher in Genesis. The Old Testament prophet Ezekiel refers to him only as a righteous man like Daniel and Job (Ezek 14:14, 20). Peter probably calls him a preacher because Noah's faith, demonstrated in his obedience to God (Gen 6:9, 22; 7:1, 5), was a proclamation of righteousness to the people of his day. This is how the writer of the book of Hebrews puts it: "By faith Noah, when warned about things not yet seen, in holy fear built an ark to save his family. By his faith he condemned the world and became heir of the righteousness that is in keeping with faith" (Heb 11:7).[74]

Through Noah's righteousness, God saved not only Noah but also his family (the "seven others" who were with him in the ark).[75] Genesis highlights Noah's righteousness and obedience, and makes it clear that all those with Noah as their representative head, or in other words, all those who were associated with Noah, escaped the judgement (Gen 6:18–21; 7:7–10).[76] In the same way, all who are in Christ are saved through him (see also Rom 5:12–19). Just as through one man's righteousness God preserved an entire family when his judgement came on those around them, so God will preserve his people today who are in Christ Jesus based on the righteousness of Christ and their association with Christ by faith.[77] Note, however, that Peter's main focus in this letter is on God's judgement on the wicked in Noah's day.

2:6–8 Example 3: The condemnation of Sodom and Gomorrah

The final example Peter cites is God's fiery judgement on *the cities of Sodom and Gomorrah*, in which there were not even ten righteous men (2:6; see Gen 18–19). The sins of these cities included violence against strangers, rape, and sexual perversion. God's judgement on them was long remembered (Isa 1:9–10; Jer 49:18; Amos 4:11; Matt 10:15). Thus they are an appropriate example for Peter to cite.

Just as he did in the previous example, Peter refers to the salvation of someone who is righteous. Abraham's nephew Lot, whom Peter describes as *a righteous man*, was saved from the destruction (2:7–8).

But in what sense was Lot a righteous man? Some suggest that the Old Testament does not portray him as such: "Lot is righteous not by example, as Genesis 19 makes clear, but by comparison to the surrounding debauchery."[78] However, this judgement may be overly severe. The fact that Lot was distressed by the evil around him suggests that he was actually a God-fearing man. However, whether he was righteous or not is not Peter's main point. The point Peter wants to make is this: If God rescued Lot, Peter's audience can take comfort as they fight against the evil of their day because God will rescue them. They can also be assured that God will not overlook the wickedness of the false teachers just as he did not overlook the sins of Sodom and Gomorrah.

An interesting point to note about the first eight verses of 2 Peter 2 is that while verses 1–3 stress that the false teachers will be condemned because of their character, verses 4–8 focus on the character of God. God is consistent in his hatred of evil and will judge it as he did in the past. The character of the false teachers merits the judgement that God's character obliges him to bring.

2:9–10 The lesson to be learnt

After the long "if" clause detailing three examples of God's judgement of the wicked, Peter draws a conclusion with a "then" clause. The NIV highlights this shift by introducing the next clause with *if this is so, then . . .* If it is true that God judged and saved in the past, then he will surely do so again. God knows how to be just to both the righteous and the ungodly.

There is also a more subtle shift in the argument as Peter reaches his conclusion. While giving the examples, his focus was on God's judgement. Now in the conclusion, he emphasizes God's deliverance. His opening point is, *the Lord knows how to rescue the godly from trials* (2:9a).[79] He is not saying that the godly will never endure trials. We may well find ourselves being persecuted, mocked, rejected and despised, but we can be sure that God will eventually deliver us in his own way and in his own time. This comforting assurance is repeated many times in the Scriptures. For example, "The righteous person may have many troubles, but the LORD delivers him out from them all" (Ps 34:19; see also 1 Cor 10:13; Rev 3:10).

The fate of the unrighteous is very different: "evil will slay the wicked" (Ps 34:21), or as Peter puts it, God knows how *to hold the unrighteous for punishment on the day of judgement* (2:9b).[80] Not all their punishment is in the future, for the Greek can also be translated as "keep the unrighteous under punishment until the day of judgement" (ESV, see also the NASB, and RSV). They are thus already enduring a measure of punishment while awaiting the great day of judgement, which will surpass all previous judgements including those on Sodom and Gomorrah (3:7; Matt 10:15; 11:24) and Tyre and Sidon (Matt 11:22; Isa 23:1–18; Ezek 28:1–26; Amos 1:9, 10). On that day God will judge every careless word (Matt 12:36) and destroy the ungodly forever with an unquenchable fire (3:7; see also 2 Thess 1:9; Isa 66:15–16; Mal 4:1).

In 2:10a Peter notes that this future judgement will come on those who, like the false teachers, pursue sinful pleasures, including sexual pleasures (2:2, 18; 3:3) and despise all authority, both human and divine, including the ultimate authority of God and Christ (2:1b).

2 Peter 2:1–10a has shown us that God has repeatedly judged the wicked and saved the righteous in the past. This consistent judgement and salvation of God in history assures believers today that God will do the same in the future. The wicked and false teachers will drink to the

dregs the cup of God's fury, while he will rescue the righteous and grant them eternal bliss because he knows what they have endured and is a specialist in saving the righteous and condemning the wicked.

Questions for Discussion

1. How does God's work in the past (history) relate to his work in the future? In what ways can we learn from biblical history as we hope for our future restoration?

2. How can you tell that a preacher, prophet or pastor is a false teacher? Are there any marks that such teachers would bear? In answering these questions, consider 2 Peter 2:1–10a, as well as Matthew 7:21–23 and Jeremiah 23:9–40.

THE DEPRAVITY AND DECEPTION OF FALSE TEACHERS

I know a man who became very angry when he was diagnosed as being HIV+ and decided that he would not die of AIDS alone. So he disguised himself as an HIV activist who was instructing people and warning them about the danger of contracting the disease. Girls assumed that someone who spoke out on these issues would not be infected himself and welcomed him into their lives, with several of them having sexual relations with him. But as the virus destroyed his immune system and he developed full-blown disease, it became obvious that he had deceived many. At his funeral I observed the life-altering and destructive effect of his depravity. Young girls he had seduced were mourning and desperately trying to convince themselves that he did not die of AIDS. But it was too late for them – they too had been infected.

This man was like the false prophets Peter condemns. While pretending to be Christians, they were infecting innocent people with the eternally destructive poison of false teaching.

2:10b–16 The Rebellion and Sensuality of the False Teachers

As a tree is known by its fruit, so the actions of false teachers expose their corrupt nature (Matt 7:18–20). Peter now goes into more detail about their evil practices. It is as if he wants to be sure that the church would be able to detect them and avoid being entrapped by them.

As the list of their vices shows, false doctrine inevitably produces immoral living. We grow in holiness and in the knowledge of God by adherence to his word. Since, however, the false teachers have forsaken the way of truth (2:15) and rejected Jesus, the Truth (2:1), it is not surprising that they have become corrupted by all kinds of vices.

The book of Proverbs reminds us that pride and insolence go together (Prov 21:24). That is exactly what we see in the false teachers who reject all external authority. They speak with pride and arrogance, presuming even to *heap abuse on celestial beings* (2:10b). These puzzling words are explained by the parallel passage in Jude 8–9, which makes it clear that the *celestial beings* are evil angels (demons). In deriding demons, these false teachers, are treading where even good angels who have God-given rights would not (2:11).

We in Africa are often very aware of spiritual forces, and so may have a better grasp of what is going on here than some Western readers. There are still some arrogant preachers in Africa who claim authority over demons, mock them, and make light of their work. We must not imitate their example. True. Christ has overcome the spirit world and we no longer need to fear its power, but that does not entitle us to speak flippantly of spiritual powers. Only fools rush in where angels fear to tread.

Arrogantly confident about their own abilities, and unwilling to learn from anyone else, false teachers are trapped in ignorance. They display it by talking derisively about things they do not understand. While they think they are superior and are becoming more and more enlightened, in reality they are becoming more and more like animals, relying on instinct rather than the knowledge of God.

While believers share in the nature of God through their knowledge of Christ (1:3–4), false teachers are more closely related to animals, and so will share the fate of beasts. We are reminded of Nebuchadnezzar of

Babylon, whom God debased because of his pride (Dan 4:30). Until he repented, he lived with beasts and ate grass like an ox (Dan 4:32). Nebuchadnezzar later repented; would that these false teachers would do so too.

False teachers may sprout like grass and flourish, but they are doomed to eternal destruction (Ps 92:7). As the book of Proverbs states, "The Lord has made everything for its purpose, even the wicked for the day of trouble" (Prov 16:4 NRSV). Peter states that they were *born only to be caught and destroyed* (2:12). They were created for capture and destruction. Their end was purposed when they were created (see also 1 Pet 2:8; Exod 9:16; Isa 54:16).[81]

The false teachers have done enormous harm, and will be treated accordingly – they will receive *harm for the harm they have done* (2:13a). They will reap exactly what they have sown (see also Job 4:8; Prov 22:8; Gal 6:7).

The false prophets are so lacking in shame that they are happy to drink and indulge in shameful practices in broad daylight; they do not even look for the cover of night (2:13b). The result is that people who are working during the day see what they are doing and are either eager to join them in their carousing or despise them for their laziness and failure to engage in honest work (John 11:9b). (Note that in Peter's day working at night was not an option, for there was no artificial light.)

The Old Testament prescribed that priests had to come from the tribe of Levi and had to be free of any physical defect (Lev 21:17–18). Similarly, any animal offered in sacrifice had to be free of any "defect or blemish" (Num 19:2; Deut 15:21; 17:1). This is the background to Peter's statement that these false teachers are *blots and blemishes* (2:13c). His point is that they are clearly unfit to serve in Christ's church, which should be spotless, holy, pure, and blameless before God (3:14; see also 1:4; Phil 1:10; 2:15).

The reference to their feasting *with you* is a reminder that such people are present among God's people. The feasting they share in would include the celebration of the Lord's Supper or Communion. False teachers eat the meal that is at the centre of the Christian faith, the feast that commemorates the death of Christ, but reject the Christ to whom the feast points. They are active in the church and enjoy Christian fellowship while continuing to sin.

Nor do these men obey Paul's instruction to Timothy to treat "younger women as sisters, with absolute purity" (1 Tim 5:2). Instead, they look at them *with eyes full of adultery* (2:14a). Unlike righteous men like Job who do all in their God-given power to resist sexual temptation (Job 31:1), these false teachers never stop looking lustfully at women, thereby committing sexual immorality in their hearts (see Matt 5:28). Today, these men would probably enjoy Internet pornography too, and when challenged would say that this is what all men do. They would argue that because African men used to have many wives, it is fine for them to have many girlfriends. But sexual sin should not be trivialized or excused; it is a symptom of a deeper problem in a person's relationship to their Saviour (2:1).

Sin is the one constant feature in the false teachers' lives: they *never stop sinning* and they seek to draw others in to sin with them as *they seduce the unstable* (2:14b), that is, those whose faith is weak. The weak need to have their faith strengthened, not have it eroded by wicked men.

Paul advised the young pastor Timothy that he should train himself in godliness (1 Tim 4:7), but these teachers are trained in greed, so that they are now *experts in greed* (2:14c). Greed is a form of idolatry (Col 3:5; Eph 4:19; 5:3) and those whose hearts are steeped in it cannot produce good fruit. That is why such people bear God's curse (Eph 2:3; Isa 57:4).

We need to remember this warning when we hear preachers who play on our greed and promise us health, wealth, and prosperity. If we start to focus on the things they promise, we are training our hearts in greed rather than in godliness. We also need to watch our own souls as we teach. Do you see opportunities to teach as a way to grow rich? Does your spiritual training involve following Paul's instructions to Timothy, or your own lust and greed?

The right way to godliness is *the straight way* (2:15a), which Peter also refers to as "the way of truth" (2:2) and "the way of righteousness" (2:21). This is the path of obedience to God (see also Ps 27:11; Prov 4:11, 26–27). Those who leave the straight path inevitably end up on some other path (Prov 2:12–13; Jer 2:13), for all of us must follow some path. The path on which these men have embarked is the same one taken by the prophet *Balaam* in the Old Testament (2:15b–16; see also Jude 11). Balaam was a prophet who wanted riches more than he wanted to obey God and was rebuked for it by the donkey he was riding (Num

22:1–41).[82] Balaam was also guilty of practising divination (Josh 13:22) and of enticing Israel into sexual sin (Num 31:16; see also Rev 2:14). Like him, the false teachers are more interested in gain than godliness and draw others into sexual sin. They too are willing to utter false prophecies if it will put money in their pockets. They have no interest in serving God's people; they want God's people to serve and enrich them. For them, Jesus is not the goal of their life but the means to their goal of wealth and self-aggrandisement.

Peter has not restrained himself as he describes these false teachers; we hear the same vehemence that characterized him in the Gospels. He is very concerned about the way these men's contempt for God and his word harms the faith of believers.

2:17–22 The Damaging Effects of False Teaching

Water is essential for life. In Peter's day, a spring would be a water source for a traveller or a village. Imagine making your way to the spring, assuming that you will find water there, and discovering that it has run dry. Or maybe you do not need to imagine this, for it is the experience of some in Africa. This is what happens in spiritual terms when people go to a false teacher. Jesus said that "rivers of living water" would flow from those who believe in him (John 7:38), but these teachers have rejected him (2:1), and consequently they are *springs without water* (2:17a). The prophet Jeremiah used a similar metaphor when he said that the people of Israel were forsaking the Lord, "the spring of living water" and digging "their own cisterns, broken cisterns that cannot hold water" (Jer 2:13). A waterless spring creates a desert, a place where people die of thirst.

It is interesting to note that the word translated "without water" is the same word Jesus used to refer to the dry places where demons wander (Matt 12:43; see also Luke 11:24). Peter may be hinting that the false teachers have something in common with demons. Unlike true teachers whose teaching is a spring of life (Prov 13:14), their teaching is empty, devoid of any spiritual benefits and demonic. They "depart from the faith by devoting themselves to deceitful spirits and teachings of demons" (1 Tim 4:1 ESV).

Using a second metaphor to reinforce his point, Peter describes the false teachers as *mists driven by a storm* (2:17b). They are like clouds that seem to promise much needed rain but are blown away by strong winds, leaving the ground parched and thirsty. What a contrast with the teaching of Moses, who prayed

> Let my teaching fall like rain
> and my words descend like dew,
> like showers on new grass,
> like abundant rain on tender plants. (Deut 32:2)

What Moses proclaimed was the word of the Lord, not his own words. And God promises that his word will bring fruit:

> As the rain and the snow
> come down from heaven,
> and do not return to it
> without watering the earth
> and making it bud and flourish,
> so that it yields seed for the sower and bread for the eater,
> so is my word that goes out from my mouth:
> It will not return to me empty,
> but will accomplish what I desire
> and achieve the purpose for which I sent it. (Isa 55:10–11)

The words of the false teachers will produce no such fruit. Their teaching does not water the soil of the heart.

Because the false teachers promise life-giving water when they have none to give and so lure others to their death, they deserve the punishment of *blackest darkness [that] is reserved for them* (2:17b).

Peter goes on to speak of how these men operate. They begin by targeting new converts, those who are *just escaping from those who live in error* (2:18c), or in other words, those who are just beginning to separate themselves from unbelievers.[83] They impress them with their boastful confidence (2:18a; see also Jude 16). New converts are often impressed by preachers who are loud, charismatic, and make great claims for themselves. The converts do not know enough to recognize when a preacher is not being faithful to the Scriptures or when high-sounding speech is empty of truth.[84]

These teachers also appeal to *the lustful desires of the flesh*, or in other words, to sensual pleasures (2:18b). These include sexual desires, but are not limited to them for the word translated "lust" refers to all kinds of sinful pleasure (Mark 4:19; John 8:44; Rom 1:24; 6:12).[85] Thus false teachers may make a display of the wealth they claim to have gained from God, showing off their gold jewellery, expensive watches, and fleet of luxury cars, and invite the weak in faith to follow them, promising that they too will enjoy these benefits. While none of these things are wrong in themselves, they become evil when they are used to encourage greed and lust in others.

To give a biblical example, there is nothing sinful about enjoying eating fish, cucumbers, melons, leeks, onions, and garlic. These are all things that God created to be enjoyed. But the desire for them became sinful when the Israelites started to say that they would rather eat these foods than follow God. They started to talk about returning to their old life as slaves in Egypt, and God punished them for it (Num 11:4–5). Similarly, the false teachers are encouraging young Christians to return to the sinful pleasures that were part of their old life as pagans – "debauchery, lust, drunkenness, orgies, carousing and detestable idolatry" (1 Pet 4:3). These are temptations that believers should resist, not give in to (1 Pet 2:11; Titus 2:12). New believers may follow such teachers, because they are still ignorant of some aspects of their new faith (1:14) – and all the more so if they are told that they have no need to fear God's judgement (3:4–6).

The false teachers promise their followers *freedom*. But this is not the same kind of freedom that Jesus and Paul speak of. That freedom is the freedom of those who have been set free from the chains of sin and so are free to serve God and one another (John 8:35–26; Gal 2:4; 5:1, 13). It is the freedom to live in obedience to God's word. But the freedom offered by the false teachers is the freedom to do whatever you want. Since these teachers have rejected all authority, including that of Christ (2:1, 10), they promise their followers similar freedom from the moral expectations of God's word. They twist Paul's teaching on freedom and use it to encourage moral laxity (3:15–16). Does this sound familiar? There are preachers today who preach only about God's love and his blessing, and never preach about sin or repentance. Isn't such preaching likely to have a similar effect to that of the false teachers?

Ironically, these preachers of freedom are themselves enslaved. Based on the general principle that *people are slaves to whatever has mastered them* (2:19b), the false teachers are "slaves of depravity" (John 8:34; Rom 6:16). By contrast, true believers are slaves of God and righteousness, and such slavery is true freedom (Rom 6:18–22). Rather than rejecting God's law, we rejoice in it.

With their boasting, appeals to vicious desires, and false promises, the false teachers are "as misleading and seductive as the hunter who attempts to catch his prey."[86] They have baited a trap with their lies, and they devour those who fall into it.

Peter's words in 2:20b are sobering. He states that those who turn their backs on whatever spiritual experience they have had end up *worse off at the end than they were at the beginning.* He is not alone in saying this, for Jesus made the same point when talking about the state of those who have been delivered from demons but then become possessed again by even more demons (Matt 12:43–45; Luke 11:24–26). This warning needs to be heard by both the false teachers and those they have deceived.

Once again, we are faced with the question of whether these people were ever true believers. The reference to their having *escaped the corruption of the world by knowing our Lord and Saviour Jesus Christ* (2:20a) suggests that they had indeed been converted. After all, Peter earlier stated that conversion comes about through knowledge of Christ (1:2–3, 8; see also 3:18). As before, opinions are divided as to whether they were ever truly Christians. My own position is that true conversion lasts a lifetime, but in the case of false faith, as in the parable of the sower, there are seeds that sprout and give evidence of spiritual life but are choked by the weeds of the world before that life truly begins (Matt 13:18–22). The fate of those of whom this is true is worse than if they had never known anything about Christ (see also Heb 6:4–6; 10:26–31).

Therefore, Peter argues in 2:21, it is better to be ignorant of the truth than to ignore it.[87] It is a terrible thing to turn your back on *the way of righteousness* (the path of obedience to God – Matt 21:32; Ps 23:3; Prov 2:8; 8:20; 12:28), for to do so is to turn your back on God. They have rejected *the sacred command,* that is, the Christian ethical teaching *that was passed on to them* (see 1 Thess 4:2; Jude 3). What was intended to transform them has ended up condemning them. Ignorance would have made their case better, but since they know the right thing to do and have failed to do it, it will be worse for them (Luke 12:47, 48; John 9:41; Jas 4:17).

It is easy to condemn the false teachers, but we would also do well to look at ourselves. Are we ignoring some aspect of the truth and preferring a lie that sin tells us? If so, we risk ending up like the false teachers and their converts. So it is wise to be alert to areas of our life in which we ourselves are ignoring God's truth.

Peter ends this section of his letter by quoting two well-known proverbs[88] that apply to the false teachers and those who follow them: "A dog returns to its vomit" and "A sow that is washed returns to her wallowing in the mud" (2:22). To get the full force of these sayings, we need to remember that both dogs and pigs were unclean animals in the Old Testament (Exod 22:31; Lev 11:7; Deut 14:8) and that this attitude continued in New Testament times (Matt 7:6; Luke 16:21; Phil 3:2). There are still many parts of the world where these animals are despised.

Peter's Jewish readers would also have been reminded of the words in the book of Proverbs: "As a dog returns to its vomit, so fools repeat their folly" (Prov 26:11). Like dogs, the false teachers and their followers have returned to the corruption they once rejected. Like pigs, they now wallow in the filth from which they were "cleansed".

Believers must read this chapter as a warning to guard against apostasy. The false teachers and their followers fell away, proving that they never really belonged to God (1 John 2:19). They were not truly saved. Those whom God saves, he keeps for eternal life because he knows how to rescue his elect from all evils (2:9; Ps 34:19).

Questions for Discussion

1. How do we distinguish between someone who disagrees with us on some points and someone who is a false teacher? Why is it important to make this distinction?

2. What form do the sins Peter was writing about take in Africa today? Would he mention other sins if he was writing to your church?

3. How does Peter seek to protect the church from the harm caused by false teachers? How should we seek to protect the church from false teachers today?

OUR CERTAIN FUTURE

My grandmother who raised me spent most of her days working hard on the farm, especially during the harvest season when she would gather enough food for us for the rest of the year. Because she was out on the farm all day, I would be home alone after school on most days of the week. This meant that I had a lot of freedom to do whatever I wanted, but I usually made sure everything was in order by the time she came home. One day, however, I was absent-minded. I had stolen some sugar from the kitchen and I hid while I ate it. Then I decided to go back for more. (You may be wondering why I would steal something as ordinary as sugar, but there were no candies readily available.)

While I was in the kitchen getting more sugar, I heard people talking outside and realized that my grandmother had returned. Normally I would have welcomed her home, but instead I ran out of the kitchen and headed off. She immediately knew that something was wrong. My aunt who was with her chased after me, caught me, and found the sugar in my pockets. She led me to my grandmother, and I was severely punished.

The greedy false teachers were like me in that they ignored the fact that someone would be returning. They had convinced themselves that the return of the Lord was unlikely to happen, and so they lived as they pleased. Peter warns the church not to follow their example, but to live in light of the imminent return of Jesus.

3:1–2 Loving Reminders

Though Peter was writing to the church about serious matters, and became heated when speaking about the false teachers, his tone is warm when he addresses his *dear friends*. The Greek word he uses can also be translated as "beloved" (ESV, NASB).[89] He repeats this word five times in this chapter – four times with reference to the people he is writing to, and one time referring to Paul as his beloved fellow apostle. In an earlier chapter, he had reminded the believers that Christ is God's beloved Son (1:17). His reason for stressing his love for the believers may be to remind them that he is not writing as a tyrant. He is not seeking to coerce them, but is warning them because he loves them and knows that they are loved by God because they love the Son of God. His willingness to declare his love for his people is a corrective for leaders who think that they show their strength by their severity.

The letter we are reading is evidently the *second letter* Peter wrote to this group (3:1a). The first is most likely 1 Peter.[90] Both were written for the same reason: to remind them of the teachings of the prophets and apostles and stimulate them *to wholesome thinking*. The life of the mind is very important for our Christian walk. If we do not think wholesomely, we may ignore the return of Christ and immerse ourselves in all kinds of evil, just as I forgot about my grandmother's return and indulged in theft.

Peter is concerned about the future of his beloved friends in Christ. Will they remain confident in what they have believed and hold firmly to the truth when their beliefs are challenged? To strengthen their confidence, he reminds them that their beliefs are rooted in *the words spoken . . . by the holy prophets and the command given by our Lord and Saviour through your apostles* (3:2; see also 1:16–20). His use of the phrase *your apostles* is another testimony to how close he was to this community – he is speaking of the apostles who actually preached to them[91] and taught them the Lord's commands, that is, Jesus' teaching (see 1 John 2:7; 3:23; 4:21; 2 John 1:4–6).[92] His reference to the prophets as *holy* may be a gentle reminder that the false teachers who are contradicting the apostles are anything but holy in their lives.

It is important to note the continuity Peter sees between the Old Testament (the holy prophets) and the New Testament (Jesus' teaching as transmitted by the apostles). It is a continuity that Paul also acknowledges

(Eph 2:20; 3:5–6; see also Luke 1:70; Acts 3:21; Heb 1:1). This is something that we need to remember. In many of our churches the Old Testament is not given much attention. Yet if Peter and Paul both saw it as foundational for our faith and expected believers to know it and remember its teachings, then surely we should also regularly preach from the Old Testament. The Old and New Testaments together comprise the Christian Scriptures. In fact the Old Testament lays the foundation for the New Testament. If we do not know the Old Testament, we cannot fully understand the New Testament.

Peter is making it very clear that both the Old Testament prophets and the New Testament apostles are trustworthy guides to our faith, provided for us by God through the Holy Spirit.

3:3–7 Warning against Doubting Christ's Return

The teachings of the prophets and apostles include warnings about what will happen in *the last days* (3:3a). These are not just the days immediately preceding Christ's return. Rather, the expression refers to the whole period from Christ death and resurrection until his return (see Acts 2:17; Heb 1:1–2; 1 Pet 1:20).[93] So the last days extend from the days in which Peter was writing to the days in which we are living until the second coming of Christ.

Certainly the prophecy that *scoffers will come, scoffing*[94] was being fulfilled then and is still being fulfilled now. "Scoffing" is not a word much in use nowadays, and so maybe we should use the words "mocking" or "ridiculing" instead. Such mockery takes different forms in different communities, but a major focus of the mockery directed at believers in Peter's day was that they were stupid to believe that Christ would actually return. Even today we find scoffers like that. Someone I attempted to evangelise said, "How can you keep believing that your Christ is coming back when he said his return would be soon, but has delayed for two thousand years plus?" Such scoffers do not understand what Scripture actually teaches, and do not care to listen to any explanation of it. They are not interested in truth but only in *following their own evil desires* (3:3b).

The scoffers Peter is talking about claim that Christ will never return, despite the fact that his promise to return is mentioned many times in the

New Testament.[95] They laugh at this belief, saying that because Christ has not yet returned he will never return. They insist that *ever since our ancestors died,*[96] *everything goes on as it has*[97] *since the beginning of creation* (3:4). The words translated *our ancestors* are literally "the fathers", and probably refer to the founding fathers of the Jewish nation, Abraham, Isaac, and Jacob (see Luke 1:72, 73; Acts 3:13, 25; Luke 1:55, 72; John 4:20; 1 Cor 10:1).[98]

The mockers argue that since things have not changed in so long a time, they will never change. But their premise is wrong, as Peter quickly points out. Things certainly have changed in the past. The first change was when God created the earth *out of water and by water* (3:5). The earth itself has not existed for ever. God caused dry land to emerge from the all-covering sea (see Gen 1:2, 6–10; Ps 24:2).[99] It may be that Peter stresses the role of water in creation because in the very next verse he speaks of the role of water in the destruction of the world at the time of the great flood (3:6).[100] The destruction of the world of that time gives credence to the prophecies of future destruction (Matt 24:37–39; Luke 17:26–27).

The mockers *deliberately forget* this history (3:5a). In this they are like many others who pick and choose the portions of Scripture that support their opinions and intentionally "forget" those that run counter their views. Maybe they have good reason to want to forget about God's judgement in the past because they themselves will face that same judgement, albeit on a larger scale, in the future (2:3).

The word that prophesied Christ's return and the coming destruction of the world is a trustworthy word. In fact it is *the same word* that first created the world (3:7; see 3:5). Now God is waiting for the right time to utter the word that will again call down judgement on the world.[101] But this time the judgement will be by fire, for God swore that he would not again destroy the earth with water (Gen 9:11).

Just as the flood destroyed all the wicked on earth, so the ungodly will be destroyed when God's judgement comes by fire. We saw a foretaste of such judgement when God destroyed Sodom and Gomorrah (Gen 19:23), and the Old Testament contains many other references to judgement by fire.[102] The New Testament also speaks of God's judgement on the world and sinners in terms of eternal fire (Matt 25:41; see also 2 Thess 1:8–9; Matt 10:15; 11:22–24).

The book of Proverbs reminds us that "penalties are prepared for mockers and beatings for the backs of fools" (Prov 19:29). That is true on both the human and divine levels. God is not passive, nor have his promises failed as the scoffers claim. He will surely bring judgement on the present cosmos and on the wicked (Rev 20:11–15). On the judgement day, the ungodly and scoffers will suffer the penalty of eternal separation from the presence of the living God (2 Thess 1:8–9).

3:8–10 God's Timing versus Our Timing

Peter exposes another flaw in the scoffers' logic when he points out that God does not see time in the same way that we do: *with the Lord a day is like a thousand years, and a thousand years are like a day* (3:8). The psalmist made the same point: "A thousand years in your sight are like a day that has just gone by, or like a watch in the night" (Ps 90:4). Psalm 90 contrasts our transience with God's eternal nature and reliability. We all return to dust, no matter how long our lifespan may be (Gen 5), and are swept away by God's anger. God, however, endures "from everlasting to everlasting", transcending time so that for him a thousand years feel no longer than a few hours in a night (Ps 90:1–6, 9). Ignoring this fact leads the false teachers to a mistaken hope that judgement will never come on them, but the believers who have the mind of Christ must not forget God's perspective. We must be vigilant lest the propaganda of the scoffers deform our thinking. Those who are surrounded by false teachers or faced with persecution should not lose heart; God will come in his time and bring an end to all persecution, suffering, and falsehood.

Peter acknowledges that from our perspective the Lord may appear to be slow to act, but he insists that what appears to be slowness on God's part is actually a sign of his compassion. In the Old Testament God sometimes delayed his judgement to allow sinners to repent (see 2 Kgs 14:25–27; Ezek 18:23, 32; 33:11), and now Peter argues that God is doing the same thing in the last days: *The Lord is not slow in keeping his promise, as some understand slowness. He is patient with you, not wanting anyone to perish, but everyone to come to repentance* (3:9).

God waits because he delights in showing mercy (see Isa 30:18; 1 Tim 1:16). He shows great patience even with "the objects of his wrath"

(Rom 9:22). However, the people Peter is addressing are believers, and so the *you* in *he is patient with you* refers to believers.[103] Peter is saying that God is patient because he does not want any of his flock to perish. As Jesus said, God has other sheep that still need to be brought into the fold (John 10:16).[104] If this is the reason for God's patience, we ought to accelerate the preaching of the gospel, which is God's chosen means of redemption, for his patience will not last forever.

When the day of the judgement does come, its arrival will be as unexpected as the breaking-in of a thief in the night (3:10). Here is the final part of Peter's answer to the scoffers. The day of the Lord will come, regardless of whether you expect it or not. When I stole the sugar as a child, my failure to consider the inevitability of my grandma's return did not mean that she would not return. Neither will the false belief of the scoffers derail the second coming of Christ.

Though we know that his coming is certain, we do not know when it will occur. When thieves break into a home, they never tell the homeowner what time they will be coming or how they plan to break in. Just as my grandma came when I did not expect her and caught me in my sin, so the day of the Lord Jesus Christ will come in an unforeseen way and at an unexpected time (see also Matt 24:42–44; Luke 12:39; 1 Thess 5:2).

In the Old Testament the day of the Lord is described as a day of salvation for the righteous and judgement for the wicked (Isa 13:6, 9; Joel 1:15; Zeph 1:7). On that day the heavens will disappear with a roar[105] from the presence of the Lord (see also Isa 34:4), likely on account of his wrath (see also Rev 6:14; 20:11; 21:1). Not only will the heavens disappear, but so will *the elements*, that is, the "substances underlying the natural world, the basic elements from which everything in the world is made and of which it is composed."[106] All these will be destroyed by a fire so intense that the mountains will melt like wax (Mic 1:4; Nah 1:5).

This is a terrifying prospect. It could happen at any moment – even while you are reading this book. We will all be surprised when it happens. But will this be a joyous surprise at the return of a loved one or the terrified surprise of those who are caught in wrongdoing and face judgement? Will we run to Christ, or will we seek to hide from him when he returns?

Questions for Discussion

1. Have you encountered scoffing within the church or in your community? What is the reason for it? Discuss the antidotes to scoffing using 2 Peter 3 as your guide.

2. Peter told the believers to remember the predictions of the Old Testament prophets and the commands of Christ. What can we do to keep their teaching in our own minds and hearts so that scoffers who come making biblically unfounded claims do not deceive us?

3. Peter also tells us that the false teachers deliberately forget great truths from the Scriptures (3:5). How can we train ourselves to listen not just to what people say but to what they do not say? How can we tell when some aspect of the truth is being ignored?

4. In what ways do you need to change the ways you plan and live your life so that your life as a whole reflects belief in the second coming of Christ?

BE HOLY

Imagine a couple who set out to buy some land that they want to turn into a farm. The land they acquire is full of rocks and stones, and they have to put in a lot of hard work clearing it. They tackle the task with enthusiasm and soon the big rocks are gone. But the removal of the big rocks reveals that there are also a great many smaller rocks. Getting rid of these is a longer and more difficult task, but the couple cling to their dream of the farm and carry on clearing them. But as they work, it becomes clear that there are also a great many small stones and pieces of gravel that will need to go before they can cultivate a good crop. Clearing them is a wearisome task, but the husband and wife persevere until eventually the soil is ready for planting. Now at last they can grow crops that will meet their own needs and help them fund their children's education.

The above story illustrates what growing in righteousness entails. When we first come to Christ, we turn away from obvious and blatant sins as we take our early steps of spiritual growth. Sad to say, many of us stop there. But like the couple in the story who kept going until they had removed even the small stones and gravel, we need to go on eliminating the little besetting sins that muddle the landscape of our lives. This is what Peter is calling on believers to do in this section of his letter where he uses words such as "holy", "spotless" and "blameless" to describe what their lives should be like.

3:11–13 In Light of the Future, Be Holy Now

In the preceding verses Peter encouraged the believers to trust the words of the prophets and apostles and denounced those who were encouraging them to doubt that Christ would actually return. He reminded them that the day of the Lord will come unexpectedly and that the world as we know it will be destroyed by fire.

This prospect should terrify the scoffers. But how should we as Christians respond to it? What difference should it make in our lives? The apostle's answer to these questions is that those who believe in Christ's return should *live holy and godly lives* (3:11). Note that Peter does not actually present this as the answer to a question but as an exclamation.[107] He is saying something like, "Since all this is going to happen, what wonderful, holy people you should be!"[108] Because we know that earthly things will not endure, we should hold on to them lightly and should concentrate on the things that will truly last, especially the pursuit of holy conduct without which we will not see the Lord (Heb 12:12).

Some people might think that eagerly anticipating Christ's return would discourage Christians from paying attention to what is happening now – and there have been some Christians of whom that is true. However, Peter's point is that our anticipation of what is going to happen in the future inspires us to do the best we can in the present and to make sure that our lives will be pleasing to Christ when he returns. When there is no anticipation of the day of the Lord, our desire for holiness and pursuit of it can be greatly weakened. Just as the couple mentioned above worked very hard because of their vision of a bright future on their farm, we too must do our best to clear from our lives anything that would keep us from participating in the new heaven and earth when they come.

Peter goes on to say that as believers grow in holy conduct and piety, they are speeding the coming of the day of God (3:12).[109] In theological terms, we could say that sanctification hastens glorification, the perfection that we will all share in at the second coming of Jesus. But what does this mean in practice? How does our holy conduct hasten the coming of the Lord?

I would suggest that one way it does this is through our eager pursuit of holy living and through prayer. Jesus taught his disciples to pray for the coming of the kingdom and that his will would be done on earth (Matt

6:10). Another way we hasten Christ's second coming is by spreading the gospel. Jesus said, "And this gospel of the kingdom will be preached in the whole world as a testimony to all nations, and then the end will come" (Matt 24:14). So our holy conduct, prayer, and the advancement of the gospel to all nations hastens the coming day of God.

This coming day of God is a day when the heavens will be destroyed and the basic components of the world will melt in the intense heat of the fire of God's wrath (3:12).[110] Believers, however, will be spared to live in a new creation that will be characterized by righteousness (3:13). Like the couple on their farm, believers will delight in their God-built home, the new heaven and new earth.

What will this new heaven and new earth be like? The prophet Isaiah gives us a glimpse of it in his description of a world of peace, harmony and justice (Isa 65:17–25). It will be a world free from wickedness, tyranny and terror (Rev 21:27; Isa 35:8; 54:14) and an eternal home for all God's people (Isa 60:21).

3:14–18a In Light of the Future, Grow in Grace and Knowledge

In the closing paragraphs of his letter, Peter again refers to those he is writing to as his *dear friends* (3:14a). These words could also be translated as "beloved" – a translation that reminds us that these people are not only loved by Peter but also by God. The instructions Peter is about to give are not imposed by a dictator; rather, they flow from love for those to whom he is writing and seek a response that flows from their love for God and for their teacher.[111]

Peter then ends his final letter with four commands that flow from all that he has been saying.[112] He uses four imperative verbs: make every effort, remember, be on guard and grow.

3:14 Make every effort to be found spotless, blameless and at peace with him

Jesus himself was spotless and blameless (1 Pet 1:19) and his followers are expected to be like him. That is what it means to be holy. We should be working hard to become more like Christ in all that we do. This requires effort, as Peter made clear in 1:3–7, and as Paul too emphasized (Phil 2:1–12). We cannot simply relax and leave it all to God.

Yet at the same time, while making *every effort* we can also be *at peace* with God and others. Being at peace with Christ and others should be a priority for believers, something we should consciously seek to maintain. The writer of Hebrews commands us to strive for peace with everyone and for holiness without which we will not see the Lord at his second coming (Heb 12:14). While we are to strive for peace, the New Testament also portrays peace as a gift from the Lord, a gift to be embraced (1 Pet 1:2b; 5:14; 2 Pet 1:2). In other words, peace with God, which should engender peace with others, is a gift we are given and must be careful to maintain. To be like Christ is to be at peace with him and to strive for peace with others, and those who are at peace with Christ need not fear his judgement.

3:15–16 Bear in mind that our Lord's patience means salvation

Once again, Peter reminds his readers of what he said earlier in the letter. While false teachers confuse the patience of God with inactivity (3:4), believers should regard it as a sign of God's compassion in offering many an opportunity for salvation (3:9). Patience is an aspect of God's character that is highlighted throughout the Old Testament, where he is often described as "long-suffering" or "slow to anger".[113] The fact that God is slow to anger is a sign of his patience, mercy and love towards the unrepentant.

Peter notes that God's patience is also a theme in the letters of *our dear brother Paul* (3:15).[114] Paul, empowered by the Holy Spirit, imparted *the wisdom that God gave him* in his letters (1:21; see also 1 Cor 2:13). He spoke of his gratitude for God's patience towards him personally, while recognizing that God's patience and kindness were intended to lead people to repentance (Rom 2:4; 9:22; 1 Pet 3:20; 1 Tim 1:16).

Given that the patience of God is an important theme in the letters of both Peter and Paul, should this not also be an important theme in our own thinking and preaching? Do we thank God for his patience with us? Or do we secretly think that because God is patient, we can continue to sin? As Peter has reminded us, that is a foolish attitude. We do not know when Christ will return, and we should be living as those who are ready for it. God knows all about your secret sins (Ps 90:8) and he will punish you for them unless you repent, taking advantage of his patience towards you.

Peter and Paul had not always been in agreement on everything (Gal 2:11–14), and so it is striking that Peter refers to Paul as his *dear brother*. Clearly, they had resolved their differences, and did not hang on to grudges despite a public disagreement. But Peter does admit that Paul's letters include *some things that are hard to understand* (3:16a).[115] Some Christians tend to ignore Peter's words here and claim that they do not need teachers, pastors, or theological education to interpret God's word because they have the Holy Spirit, the teacher of all truth, who interprets it for them. This kind of thinking has led to much false teaching.

Many preachers in Africa do not spend any time reading the works of other believers and do not even attempt to receive theological education. Yet if even the Apostle Peter found Paul's letters hard to understand, surely we do too? So we should seek the help of gifted and well-trained interpreters as we try to understand them.

You may have the Spirit, but his presence in your life does not make you self-sufficient, especially when it comes to Bible interpretation. The Spirit who is in you is the same Spirit who has gifted some in the church to be teachers, to train others in the truth until we all attain maturity, unity of the faith, and knowledge of Christ (Eph 4:11–12). Some portions of Scriptures are difficult, and we must humble ourselves and seek guidance from those whom God has gifted with the task of teaching Scriptures.

Those who fail to admit that some parts of Scriptures are difficult to interpret distort them and mislead the unlearned and new converts (see 2:14). This is not a minor matter. Peter states that distorting or twisting the teachings of the apostles is an offence that merits *destruction* (3:16c). So those of us who teach should be very concerned to avoid doing this. Peter's words should drive us to careful study to make sure that we are not among those who are twisting the teachings of Scriptures. Now we understand James's warning that "not many of you should become teachers, my fellow believers, because you know that we who teach will be judged more strictly" (Jas 3:1). Misleading others is a serious matter in God's eyes.

We may be surprised to hear Peter refer to Paul's letters as standing alongside *the other Scriptures* (3:16b). This is an important point we should not miss. Peter is treating Paul's writing as having the same authority as the Old Testament Scriptures, and sharing the same divine inspiration. Clearly Paul's letters were being read in the churches, just as the Old Testament was read in the synagogues. The believers recognized that God's Spirit spoke though him.[116]

3:17 Be on your guard against error

Once again, Peter refers to his readers as his *dear friends* as he issues his final instructions. He begins them with the word *therefore* indicating that he is drawing an inference from the argument introduced with the word "since": *since you have been forewarned*. Throughout his letter Peter has been warning his readers about false teachers and their destructive teaching that promotes ungodliness. Here he refers to their teaching as *the error of the lawless* (3:17; see also 2:7). The term translated *the lawless* could also be rendered "the wicked" (KJV) and "unprincipled men" (NASB, NET). These are people who do not have any authority over their lives, in other words, they refuse to allow God's word to govern their lifestyles.

Peter's readers have been *forewarned*[117] – not only by his letter but also by the Old Testament prophets and the apostolic teaching in general. In light of the facts that Christ will return and that false teachers are to be expected, believers must brace themselves to be ready for the one and to resist the other so that they are not carried away by error but instead retain their *secure position*.[118] If we lose our footing on the solid ground of scriptural truth, we will fall away from the faith into apostasy (see also Gal 5:4; Rom 11:11; Heb 4:11).[119]

Elsewhere, Peter teaches that God guards believers for future salvation (1 Pet 1:5; see also John 17:15; 2 Thess 3:3; Jude 24), but this does not lessen the need for believers to be on guard against the danger of falling. Rather, we should work harder because God has worked and is working for us (see 1 Cor 15:10; Phil 2:12–13; Heb 13:20–21).

3:18a Grow in grace and knowledge

At the beginning of this letter, Peter prayed for those he was writing to, saying "Grace and peace be yours in abundance through the knowledge of God and of Jesus our Lord" (1:2). Now, at the end of the letter, he commands them to *grow in the grace and knowledge of our Lord and Saviour Jesus Christ* (3:18a). This is an interesting example of the relationship between work and prayer. Peter's prayer for them did not mean that his readers did not have to work to grow in grace. Prayer does not short-circuit the command to grow in grace; rather, it energizes it.

But how do we set about growing in grace? According to 1:2, we gain grace through our knowledge of the grace-giving Saviour, Jesus Christ. Thus, the more intimate our knowledge of Christ, the more grace we experience. But this knowledge, although commanded, is something only God can give. Israel failed to know because God did not grant them hearts to understand (Deut 29:4). Both David and Solomon prayed that God would grant them knowledge (1 Kgs 3:9; 4:29; Pss 19:34; 73; 125; 130; 144; 169). Jesus told his disciples that they had "been given to know the secrets of the kingdom" (Luke 8:10). John said the Son of God is the one who gives knowledge of God and of himself (1 John 5:20). Paul prayed that God would give the churches knowledge (Eph 1:17). It is indeed from the mouth of the Lord that knowledge of the Lord comes (Prov 2:6). So the grace and knowledge that Peter commands are gifts of God for which we must pray.

3:18b Conclusion

When we experience God's grace and grow in our knowledge of him, we are moved to praise. And so Peter's final words in this letter are a doxology or hymn of praise: *To him be glory both now and forever!* (3:18b).

What is unusual about this doxology is that the *him* clearly refers to "our Lord and Saviour Jesus Christ" (3:18a). Doxologies are normally addressed only to God, and so Peter is ending his letter, as he began it, with a clear statement of the deity of Christ.[120]

Christ is worthy of glory both in the present age and in the age to come. He alone is worthy of eternal praise, and eternal life is to know him (John 17:3). To him, therefore, *be the glory both now and forever, Amen!*

Questions for Discussion

1. Peter says that because of the promise of a new heaven and new earth we are to make every effort to be spotless and blameless (3:14). What would a blameless and spotless life look like in the context of your

church, marriage, family, business, and education? How should 2 Peter 3:14 influence our day-to-day lifestyle?

2. In what practical ways can you pursue growth in grace and knowledge of our Lord Jesus Christ as Peter commands in 2 Peter 3:18?

3. Despite writing under the inspiration of the Holy Spirit, the Apostle Paul wrote some things that are difficult to understand. Why does God inspire difficult passages, and what should be your approach to such passages? Consider the following Scriptures in discussing this question: 1 Corinthians 2:14; Psalm 119:18; Proverbs 2:1–6; 2 Timothy 2:7.[121]

JUDE

INTRODUCTION

Jude, the second-to-last book in the Bible, is one of the shortest books in the New Testament, and one of the most neglected. From the time when I was converted till today, I cannot remember having heard any African preacher do a series on the book of Jude. At most, the concluding section of the book is used as a benediction at the end of worship services.

There are several reasons for Jude's neglect. The first is its brevity – in the original Greek, it totals a mere 452 words. Only Philemon (335 words), 2 John (245 words), and 3 John (218 words) are shorter. A second reason is that, unlike other letters in the New Testament, it refers to obscure and problematic works like *1 Enoch* and the *Assumption of Moses*. A third and final reason for its neglect is its focus on judgement, which may not be appealing to those more accustomed to prosperity preaching. Even faithful preachers prefer books that deal with the love of God rather than the judgement of God.

Yet, like the other books of the Bible, the book of Jude was inspired by God's Spirit, and so we must study it, learn from it, and use it to train ourselves in righteousness. Jude is rich with soul-encouraging and faith-keeping truths. It reminds us that God is able to keep his people from stumbling and to present them before himself blameless on the last day (v. 24). There could not be a better message than this! Those whom God is keeping will stand faultless before the throne of God while unbelievers and those who distort and despise the truth of this book and the rest of Scripture will be judged and condemned.

Date

Our understanding of when this letter was written is affected by who we think wrote it. The author identifies himself simply as "Jude, a servant of Jesus Christ and brother of James" (v. 1). If this James is the brother of our Lord Jesus, as I will show later, then Jude is also Jesus' blood brother. In that case, Jude must have been written some time in the first century. Moreover, if 2 Peter made use of Jude, as is generally accepted among students of the Scriptures,[1] and 2 Peter was written by the Apostle Peter, then Jude must have been written before Peter's death, which places it around AD 65.

There is nothing in the letter that suggests a later date. The false teaching addressed in the book would have been common in Jude's day.

ADDRESS AND BLESSING

When we receive a message, whether in the form of a letter, text, email or voicemail, our response is affected by who the author is and what we think of the author. If we identify it as junk mail, we delete the text or email or throw the envelope away unopened. But if the message comes from someone we love and respect, we eagerly read the letter. Authorship matters in all communication.

The Author

The author of the letter identifies himself as *Jude*, a variation of the name "Judas", which is the Greek form of the Hebrew name "Judah", meaning, "Praise the Lord". In the New Testament there are six men who have this name: (1) Judas Iscariot, who betrayed Jesus and is placed last in the list of the apostles in all the gospels;[2] (2) Judas the Galilean (Acts 5:37); (3) Judas, whose house Paul stayed in after his experience on the Damascus road (Acts 9:7–12); (4) Judas who is also called Barsabbas (Acts 15:22, 27, 32); (5) Judas the apostle, who is referred to as the son of James and is listed among the disciples after James the son of Alphaeus and Simon the Zealot (Luke 6:16; John 14:22; Acts 1:13); and (6) Judas who is one of Jesus' brothers (Matt 13:55; Mark 6:3). Which of these is most likely to be the man who identifies himself as *a brother of James* (v. 1b)?

We can answer that question by a process of elimination. Judas Iscariot died long before the possible date of this letter. Judas the Galilean, the Judas with whom Paul stayed, and Judas Barsabbas are such minor characters that their names would have carried no authority, so it is unlikely that this letter came from them. Judas the apostle could be the author, but if he were, he would most likely have described himself as an apostle, not merely as James' brother. That leaves the Judas whom the people in Jesus' hometown identify, along with James, as one of Jesus' brothers.[3]

He is the one whom some of the early church fathers regarded as the author of this letter. For example, Clement of Alexandria said,

> Jude was the brother of the sons of Joseph, but despite his relationship to the Lord, he did not say that he was Jesus' brother. What did he say? He called himself Jude, the servant of Jesus Christ, that is, of the Lord, and the brother of James, who was the Lord's brother.[4]

But how can we be sure that this "James" whom Jude mentions is the brother of Christ? Once again, we can use a process of elimination. There are at least four men named James in the New Testament. One of them was the disciple who was put to death in the early years of the church (Acts 12:2). Then there were James the father of Alpheus (Mark 3:18; 15:40) and James the father of Judas (Luke 6:16; Acts 1:13) – but these men are obscure figures, whereas Jude's confident reference to his brother James suggests that James must have been someone who was well known. The only other option is James the brother of Christ, who was a leader of the church in Jerusalem (Acts 15:13–21; Gal 1:19; 2:9). He would have been very well known in the early church, and so it would have been likely that Jude would identify himself as "James' brother" without any further explanation.

Of course, Jude could also have called himself Jesus' brother, but that was not how he saw his primary relationship to Jesus. He describes himself as *a servant of Jesus Christ* (v. 1a). Christ is more his master than his blood brother. Like a servant, Jude is submissive to his master and focused on obeying him and carrying out his instructions. In declaring that he is a servant of Christ, Jude asserts that he submits to Christ, belongs to Christ, obeys Christ, and owes his all to him. But at the same time, he is aligning himself with the great servants of God in the Old Testament like Abraham (Gen 26:24; Deut 9:27; Ps 105:6, 42), Isaac (Exod 32:13; Deut 9:27), Jacob (Exod 32:13; Deut 9:27; Isa 41:8), Moses (Num 12:7; 1 Chr 6:49; 2 Chr 24:9; Neh 10:29; Dan 9:11), David (1 Kgs 11:32; Jer 33:26), Elijah (1 Kgs 18:36) – men who were totally devoted to serving Yahweh.

The fact that Jude also identifies himself in terms of his relationship to his blood brother James shows that our heavenly connection with Jesus does not mean that we should dissociate ourselves from our earthly blood relatives. On the contrary, our heavenly focus and servanthood to Christ should bring stability and greater depth to our earthly relationships (see also 1 John 3:17; 4:20–21).

The Audience

It is difficult to establish those to whom Jude writes because he only identifies his readers theologically as *those who have been called, who are loved in God the Father and kept for Jesus Christ* (v. 1c).[5] We can deduce that they were Christians, but cannot ascertain where they lived, or whether they were Jews or Gentiles, or a mix of both.

Jude describes his audience primarily by their relationship with God as people who have been *called*, *loved* and *kept*. The "call" could refer to God's general invitation to salvation (Matt 22:14), or a call to a role in the church, (Rom 1:1; 1 Cor 1:1), or the specific and effective call of God that brings people to salvation (Rom 1:6; 8:28, 30; 1 Cor 1:2). Jude uses it in the latter sense, meaning that those to whom he is writing, whether Jews or Gentiles (1 Cor 1:24), have been called by God to belong to Jesus (Rom 1:6, 7), to be his holy people (Rom 1:7; 1 Cor 1:2) and to fulfil God's purposes (Rom 8:28). This calling originates with God, or in other words, God makes the first move. As H. Wayne House says, the call of God "is issued by the Father and made effective by the work of the Holy Spirit as He illuminates and enables the individual to understand and respond positively to the Gospel of the Lord Jesus as contained in the Word of God."[6]

Jude's readers are also *loved in God the Father*. This means that it is *in* God that believers are loved; God loves only those who are in God by faith in Christ Jesus. Although the New Testament seldom describes believers as loved *in God*, it does say that believers can be in God. For example, Paul identifies the church as those in God (1 Thess 1:1; 2 Thess 1:1). The Greek could also be translated as "loved by God the Father" (HCSB, KJV). This rendering means that the believers are objects of God the Father's love.

In the New Testament, God's love for believers is a giving love. Paul says, God "loved us and gave us eternal comfort and good hope through grace" (2 Thess 2:16). We are also told that God loved us and gave us his beloved Son (John 3:16; see also Rom 8:32). God's love overflows in great generosity to the objects of his affections.

Jude underscores the tenderness of God's love by calling God *Father*. As a father, God is compassionate (Matt 6:1, 4, 6), he knows and meets the needs of his children (Matt 6:8, 11; 7:11), he forgives their sins (Matt 6:12, 14), and he will finally bring them to his kingdom in which they will shine like the stars forever (Matt 13:41).

God, who is himself love (1 John 3:16), never stops loving his beloved. He loves believers not because they deserve to be loved but because he is merciful and loving (Deut 7:6–8). Such love should move us to worship and obedience, while giving us confidence when we turn to him, secure in the knowledge that he will never reject us.

Finally, Jude says that his readers are *kept for Jesus Christ*. The question that arises is: Kept by whom? By God. What for? For Jesus Christ? In other words, God the Father sustains believers to present them to his Son as his bride.

Some translations, however, render this phrase as "kept in Jesus Christ" (KJV) or "kept by Jesus Christ" (HCSB, NET). The former means that the place or person in whom God keeps the believers is Christ. The latter means that Jesus is the one who keeps the believers. While these last two translations are valid based on the Greek, most English versions have "kept for Jesus Christ" (NET, NRSV, NIV, ESV, NASB).[7]

How does God keep his people for his Son? He guards them by sustaining the faith in Christ that he himself has given them (Phil 1:29; 1 Pet 1:5). While he reserves utter darkness for those who distort the gospel of Jesus Christ (v. 13; 2 Pet 2:17), he maintains an inheritance in heaven for believers (1 Pet 1:4) and preserves them blameless (1 Thess 5:23), so that they will enjoy that inheritance.

So be encouraged if you are in a dark season in your walk with the Lord. Keep fighting the fight of faith because God is faithful and will sustain and keep you. He will never forsake you. He has called you. He has loved you. He will always love you. He will keep you, bearing you in his mighty saving arms to the end of your days or the end of the age.

The Appeal

Those we love we bless, and that is what Jude does when he prays, *Mercy, peace and love be yours in abundance* (v. 2). He appeals to God to show mercy, peace, and love to the believers. Although the believers have already been loved by God, Jude still asks God to multiply his love, mercy, and peace to them. This is a prayer that we need ourselves, and which we in turn should pray for others.

The first thing Jude prays for is mercy, God's mercy. Paul describes God as rich in mercy (Eph 2:4), which is why we are saved (Titus 3:5; 1 Pet 1:3). God does not treat us as we deserve and reaches out to us despite our sinfulness and the sinfulness around us (v. 21; see also 2 Tim 1:18). His mercy is offered to those who fear him (Luke 1:50, 78; Heb 4:16), who are also described as vessels or objects of mercy (Rom 9:23). We should respond to such mercy with praise (Rom 15:9).

Jude also prays for peace. *Peace* is God's gift of confidence in the finished work of Christ for us (see also Rom 5:1; 15:13). It is easy for us to become restless because of our weaknesses, but we are to trust the finished work of Christ for our salvation and rest in the peace that he gives. Ultimately, Jesus is our peace (Eph 2:14). The wicked do not have such peace (Isa 48:22; 57:21; Jer 16:5), but God through Jesus Christ grants peace abundantly to his covenant people (John 14:27). Do you know the peace that comes from trusting in Christ alone for salvation?

Finally, Jude desires that God would multiply love to the believers. *Love* is the reason God is so generous to us (John 3:16; Eph 2:4). As Arthur Pink noted, "Calvary is the supreme demonstration of Divine love. Whenever you are tempted to doubt the love of God, Christian reader, go back to Calvary."[8] The love you may have from your wife, husband, fiancé, mother, father, brother, or sister cannot be compared to God's love displayed at Calvary. Do not let human relationships distract you from God's glorious and unfailing love.

Jude prayed for mercy, peace, and love because he knew that only God could give them.[9] God demonstrated this when he sent his Son to the cross. The bloodstained cross, which is the apex of the display of human hatred for God, is surprisingly also the apex of God's mercy, peace, and love for humankind. Like Jude, we should pray that God would multiply and expand the effects of his mercy, peace and love on us and others, because there is no true mercy, no true peace and no true love apart from God.

Questions for Discussion

1. Why is it important that the mercy, peace, and love of God be multiplied to believers who are faced with false teaching?

2. When have you particularly experienced the riches of God's mercy, peace or love? Share with a group about it, and unite with them to worship God for his kindness.

3. What would it mean for you to pray for God's mercy, peace and love for the people you serve, for your friends, co-workers, wife, children, brothers, sisters, uncles, aunts, nieces and nephews? Can you model for others what that means?

4. What does the way Jude introduces himself teach us about family relationships and our relationship with God?

CONTEND FOR THE FAITH

Africa once produced famous Christian theologians like Tertullian, Athanasius and Augustine. But we should not look only to the distant past when naming great African church leaders. We should also remember the names of modern African leaders who have contended for the faith.

One such man was Byang Kato, a Nigerian theologian whom God called home in 1975. He advocated for an African theology rooted in Scripture and lamented the lack of attention to God's word as the only source of theology. He denied all attempts to root African theology in African Traditional Religion:

> Unfortunately, many theologians spend their time defending African traditional religions and practices that are incompatible with biblical teaching. Some recent writers have sought to justify pagan initiation rites . . . The burning desire to defend African personality is given precedence over Scriptural injunction.[10]

One wonders what Kato would say today to the church in Africa. He would undoubtedly have urged all false preachers to stop spreading their falsehoods. He would say what he said in his day:

> In our effort to express Christianity in the context of the African, the Bible must remain the absolute source. It is God's Word addressing Africans and everyone else within their cultural

background . . . It is only as the Bible is taken as the absolute Word of God that it can have an authoritative and relevant message for Africa.[11]

It is my prayer that men like Kato would stir us up to contend for the faith that was once for all delivered to us. I would join my voice with Kato's, who prayed:

> May the Lord help us all to experience the life of Christ, stand by his sure Word of truth, and proclaim it firmly and unmistakably throughout our continent, so that Africa may hear the voice of him who is saying, "Come to me, all who labour and are heavy laden, and I will give you rest." (Matthew 11:28)[12]

Pray with me that God would answer Byang Kato's prayer in our day and ward off the poisonous and unbiblical teaching that is spreading rampantly in Africa. May we contend for the truth of God's word to preserve it for future generations.

Verse 3 A Call to Contend for the Faith

After praying for blessings on those to whom he writes, Jude addresses them as his *dear friends* ("beloved" in the ESV, NASB, RSV). It is striking that in such a short letter Jude uses this form of address three times (vv. 3, 17, 20). He obviously cares deeply about them and sees them in a special light. In the New Testament the word translated *dear friends* is used only when referring to Jesus, the only beloved Son of God (Matt 3:17; 12:18; 17:5; Mark 1:11; 9:7; 12:6; Luke 3:22; 20:13; 2 Pet 1:17) and to his followers who, like Isaac in the Old Testament (Gen 22:2, 12, 16), are called beloved "children of promise" (Gal 4:28), precious to God.[13]

When talking to dear friends, we usually want to exchange good news with them. So it was natural that what Jude would have liked to write about was the *salvation we share* (v. 3a). He uses a present tense verb (*share*) not a future tense (will share) because he sees salvation as something we already enjoy in the present, not something we will only enjoy after death. And he sees it as something that all believers share – not something that is reserved for any so-called "spiritual elite". By using the word *we* he puts himself on the same level with all the believers in Christ (see also 2 Pet 1:1). In the early church this understanding that all Christians share a common salvation moved believers to share everything else as well, including their possessions (Acts 2:44; 4:32). No wonder Jude was eager to write a letter celebrating salvation.

Although he desired to write about the shared redemption of all believers, circumstances have forced Jude to abandon his original plan. The purpose of the letter has changed. Jude's goal is to urge them *to contend for the faith* that has been given to them (v. 3b). Today *contend* is a word that is usually used in the context of sport, where two teams contend for a trophy. It means to put one's heart into accomplishing something, working hard to achieve it in the face of strong opposition. By using the word *contend*, Jude is warning his readers that what he is asking of them will not be easy but demands exertion.

While the focus in Jude 3 is on protecting the truth from corruption by falsehood, such vigilance and striving marks all of the Christian life, which is also described in the New Testament as a life of war. Jesus himself told his followers to "make every effort to enter through the narrow door" (Luke 13:24). Paul speaks of how he strenuously contends for the gospel as he seeks to bring people to faith and to maturity in their faith (Col 1:29) and he asks the Christians in Rome to pray for him as he struggles to do this (Rom 15:30). He also assures the Christians in Colossae that Epaphras wrestles in prayer for them (Col 4:12). The writer of the letter to the Hebrews speaks solemnly when he says that the struggle against sin may involve Christians shedding their own blood (Heb 12:4). Clearly, the idea of the "good fight of the faith" (1 Tim 6:12; see also 2 Tim 4:7) recurs regularly in the New Testament.

What the believers are to contend for is *the faith that was once for all entrusted to God's holy people* (v. 3c).[14] Here and in verse 20 *the faith* refers to the truths of the gospel, enshrined in the Bible, which God has entrusted to those who trust in Christ.

When we entrust something to someone, we put it into their care and protection. Usually it is something important to us, something of value. Sometimes we entrust persons into the care of others, for example, children, the sick or the elderly. God has entrusted the faith to his people, the church, so they have a great responsibility.

It is worth noting that Jude does not speak just of "God's people" but of *God's holy people* – an expression commonly rendered as "the saints". In the New Testament, a "saint" is not someone who has been officially canonized by the church because they have lived a particularly holy life. Rather, a saint is anyone whom God has set apart for himself. In other words, a saint is anyone whom God has reserved for himself and for his service.[15] In this sense, all Christians are saints, set apart by God, and so all are charged by Jude to fight for the preservation of the faith.

Contending for the faith is not optional. It is imperative because there are many who are fighting to pervert the faith. False teaching is spreading like wildfire in the churches of Africa, and God has entrusted us with the task of defending the biblical faith. Paul contended for the faith, he passed the same challenge to Timothy (1 Tim 6:12) and now the same challenge comes to us. Are we "striving together as one for the faith of the gospel"? (Phil 1:27).

We should contend for the faith both inside and outside of the church, or in other words, we must work hard to ensure that what is taught within the church is sound doctrine and that the gospel proclaimed to outsiders is the true gospel.

Note that contending for the faith in the local churches that are our covenant communities does not mean taking violent action to expel those who oppose the truth from the church. This is what Christians have sometimes done, and it is wrong. Rather, we contend for the faith by guarding the teachings of Scripture, keeping them unadulterated by falsehood. This may sometimes mean that we excommunicate a false teacher from a local church, but such actions should never be violent and should be driven by love for the one being excommunicated.

Verse 4 Why the Call Is Issued

The reason Jude needed to issue a call to contend for the faith was that some people had *secretly slipped* into the church and were spreading false teaching. Jude makes four statements about these infiltrators:

Their condemnation was written long ago (v. 4a). The passive *was written* presupposes God as the subject. God wrote the condemnation of the infiltrators long ago. God has marked false teachers for destruction. God knows these enemies of the faith, and he will condemn them forever (see also Mark 12:40; Luke 20:47; Rom 2:2). God is not taken by surprise, and he did not want his people to be taken by surprise. That is why he foretold that such people would attempt to infiltrate his church and foretold their condemnation (vv. 17–18; see also Matt 24:11; Acts 20:29–30). The presence of false teachers does not mean that the situation is out of control: "The Lord works out everything to its proper end – even the wicked for a day of disaster" (Prov 16:4).

They are ungodly people (v. 4b). Ungodliness is the inevitable result of false teaching since error does not set people free from sin. Only the truth sets free. You cannot teach unbiblically and live biblically because falsehood enslaves. An ungodly person is someone whose attitudes and agendas are contrary to those of the kingdom of God. They do not live in step with the gospel of God or the commands of God. They do not respect God or his word, which they pervert and distort for their own selfish ends. As Scripture reminds us, all the ungodly will face eternal divine judgement (Ps 37:38; Rom 1:18; 1 Tim 1:9; 2 Pet 2:5–6; 3:7). If you are like these infiltrators and do not repent, divine and eternal condemnation will also be your fate.

They pervert the grace of our God into a license for immorality (v. 4c). The infiltrators think that because God is gracious and merciful, they can ignore him and live as they please. In doing this, they are acting like children who misinterpret their parents' kindness as weakness and so carry on sinning, assuming that their parents will always show mercy. I have seen this type of thinking at work in the life of someone whom I will call Ved (not his real name). He was once a member of a local church, but these days he is involved in sexual immorality, ancestor worship, and animism. When confronted about this, he says that if God is truly gracious, then God will be merciful to him at the end and rescue him. He argues that if God intends for him to be saved, then he will be saved, no matter what he does.

There are many people who think like Ved. They use the graciousness of God as an excuse for free and lawless living. They ignore God's justice and consequently drift farther and farther away from him. The people Jude describes in these verses are on a path to destruction.

The mere fact that people can think of God's graciousness as a license for sin indicates that the gospel is indeed a gospel of grace. If the Bible taught that we must earn our salvation by our good behaviour, this type of error would never have arisen. Muslims, for example, do not think that they can ignore God's commands with impunity. Ironically, it is only because God is gracious that people can pervert his grace. He shows us kindness that we do not deserve, and, unlike the infiltrators, our response ought to be one of love, gratitude, obedience, and a desire to be like him (see also Rom 5:20–6:4).

They deny Jesus Christ our only Sovereign and Lord (v. 4d).[16] *Sovereign* and *Lord* are titles used for God the Father (Gen 15:8; Isa 1:24; Jer 1:6; Dan 9:15; Luke 2:29; Rev 6:10). When Jude uses these titles about Jesus, he indicates that he is convinced that Jesus is God, and is in fact the same as the God in the Old Testament. That is why Jude can say that Jesus saved his people from Egypt when the Old Testament says God did (v. 5). Jesus is the same as the I AM who delivered Israel (Exod 3:13–17). Jesus is God Almighty!

Jude also refers to Jesus by his title *Christ*, which means "the Anointed One" or "the Messiah" (see Ps 2:2; Matt 16:16). The false prophets deny the sovereign Lord, our Anointed Messiah. To deny the Son of God, the Messiah, is to deny God the Father (1 John 2:23). Thus the false teachers have no relationship with God because they have rejected his Son.

In what way did these people deny Christ? We know that there are some who deny Christ by saying that Jesus is not God or by refusing to accept much of his teaching. The false teachers Jude was writing about must have been less blatant in their denial of him, for Jude says that they had *secretly slipped in* (v. 4). So their denial of the Sovereign Lord of the church must have been subtle. In the context of this letter, it seems likely that it related to their attitude to God's grace. They were denying Christ by failing to submit their lives to his rule. They may have made great claims about what they believed, but their lifestyles did not match their words.

There are still people who think that their Christian faith need not affect how they live. Provided they go to church on Sunday, they feel free to sin for the rest of the week. Such people are the descendants of those Jude was writing about. So are the people who think that they can buy forgiveness by making a large donation to a preacher or to a church building project while continuing to exploit their workers. As believers who are called to contend for the faith, we must speak out against such behaviour. People who act like this are abusing the grace of God and bringing his name into disrepute.

Verses 5–7 Why the Call Matters

Some people may think that the presence of false teachers is a minor matter. Jude does not agree. So he reminds his readers of three examples of the disastrous consequences of the type of wilful disobedience to God exemplified by the teachers.

The NIV translation, *Though you already know all this, I want to remind you* (v. 5a) is not quite as accurate as the more literal NASB rendition: "Now I desire to remind you, though you know all things once for all." The phrase "know all things" makes it clear that the readers knew many more stories about God's salvation and judgement than those Jude mentions: "Their knowledge extends beyond the cautionary stories from sacred history about to be cited, and includes the fullness of God's revelation, all that a Christian can need."[17]

The fact that Jude assumes his readers know about these incidents suggests that some of them must have come from a Jewish background or have been exposed to the Jewish Scriptures, since all the examples are from the Old Testament.

Even though his readers know these stories, Jude still needs to retell them because it is so easy to forget the things that matter (see 2 Pet 1:12–15). He wants to show them that God's past acts of judgements are still relevant today. Knowing history helps us understand the present and be better prepared for the future. That is why in both the Old Testament and the New Testament, God's people are often urged to remember what God has done (Deut 5:15; 7:18; 8:2; Eph 2:11–12; 1 Cor 15:1).

Verse 5 Judgement on unbelieving Israel

The first example of divine judgement that Jude mentions is the destruction of the Israelites who failed to trust God's promises. Jude reminds his readers, *the Lord at one time delivered his people out of Egypt, but later destroyed those who did not believe* (1:5). One of the instances of

Israel's faithlessness occurred when Moses sent twelve spies to survey the promised land before Israel took possession of it. When the spies came back, Caleb and Joshua gave a good report on what they had seen (Num 13:30–33). But the report of the other spies prompted the people to grumble and refuse to trust Yahweh (Num 14:1–4, 11). Despite Moses and Aaron's pleas, Yahweh judged the people, declaring that none of those who refused to believe his promise would enter the promised land. They would all die in the wilderness (Num 14:13–23; 26–38). This story warns us that God will judge his own people if they deny him by refusing to trust and obey him – which is exactly what the ungodly individuals in Jude's time were doing.

If you compare Bible translations when you study the Scriptures, you will notice one interesting difference in the translation of Jude 5. Some translations say that it was "the Lord" who delivered Israel from Egypt, and others like the ESV say "Jesus" delivered them.[18] You may be surprised by that translation since Jesus was born in Bethlehem centuries after Moses' day. But, as we noted earlier, Jude is convinced that Jesus and God are one. In verse 4, he gives Jesus the same title attributed to Yahweh in the Old and New Testaments. Moreover, other New Testament writers also recognized that Christ existed and was active before his incarnation. The Apostle John says that Isaiah saw the pre-incarnate Christ (John 12:41). The author of Hebrews affirms that Moses suffered with Christ and for Christ (Heb 11:26). Peter affirms that the Spirit of Christ spoke through the prophets concerning the sufferings of Christ (1 Pet 1:11). Paul also says that Christ is the Rock that followed the Israelites when they were brought out of Egypt (1 Cor 11:26). Jude agrees with these other biblical writers that Christ is God and was involved in human affairs even before he came to earth as a human infant. Thus there is no problem in saying that Jesus, who is God, delivered Israel from Egypt (see also Exod 6–14).

But the same Jesus who saved Israel from Egypt also destroyed those who did not continue in faith because "they despised the pleasant land, having no faith in his promise" (Ps 106:24). It is important to note that the divine judgement mentioned in Jude 5 came on all who failed to continue trusting God, not only on the unbelieving spies. Similarly, the warning is for all who do not trust Christ, not just the infiltrators. Jude is warning the entire church to watch against unbelief.

Perhaps you may recall praying to "receive Jesus", as is the practice in some places, or perhaps you were baptized as an adult or as an infant. We are right to celebrate such occasions, but they are only the beginning. Those who have once trusted Christ must continue to trust him throughout life to be saved at the end.

While true believers cannot lose their salvation, such warnings are needed to encourage true believers to persevere. When a mother warns her son that if he puts his hand in the fire it will be burned, she is not expecting him to put his hand in the fire. The warning is meant to keep the child from doing so. In a similar fashion, God's warnings are meant to keep us from wrecking our faith. Believers in Christ can endure to the end with the help of warnings like these because, unlike Israel, whose hearts were uncircumcised (Deut 29:4; see also Deut 10:16), our hearts have been circumcised (Col 2:11; Deut 30:6) so that we can respond properly to warnings and so continue in faith. Those who are truly saved continue in faith to the end and will be saved (Mark 13:13). Those who fall away only prove that they were not believers (1 John 2:19).

Just as the Pharisees could not presume that they were saved because they were descendants of Abraham (Matt 3:9), so we cannot find assurance of our salvation by simply belonging to the right community; we must believe and continue in faith to be saved.

Verse 6 Judgement on fallen angels

The second example of divine judgement concerns the fallen angels. God judged the angels who did not stay within the limits he had set. They had abandoned the privileged *positions of authority* God had given them (Job 1:6) and moved into places where they had no right to be. These "angels" were probably the fallen angels who possessed men and through them married women before the flood (Gen 6:1–4; 2 Pet 2:4).[19] Because of their rebellion, God has kept these fallen angels in eternal chains under thick darkness until the great judgement day (2 Pet 2:4, 17; Acts 2:20; 1 Thess 5.2, Rev 6:17; 16:14).

Jude uses a word play on the word *keep* to stress this point: The angels *did not keep* their God-assigned position and now find themselves *kept* for judgement. They did not keep themselves from evil, and so God is now keeping them in chains. Hell was prepared for these angels (Matt 25:41), and they will suffer there forever (Rev 20:2).

Jude's point is that if even angels cannot escape God's judgement when they rebel, neither will ungodly humans.

Verse 7 Judgement on Sodom and Gomorrah

The third example of historical judgement mentioned by Jude is the destruction of "Sodom and Gomorrah and the surrounding towns" (Gen 19:24–25). The inhabitants of these cities indulged in such evil practices that even though Abraham interceded for them, God destroyed them by fire, sparing only Lot (Gen 18–19). This judgement is often referred to in both the Old and New Testaments (Deut 29:23; Isa 1:9; 13:19; Amos 4:11; Matt 10:15; 2 Pet 2:6). It serves as a sign of the coming fiery judgement on all the wicked cities of the world.

Jude says that the judgement on the people of Sodom and Gomorrah is *an example of those who suffer the punishment of eternal fire* (v. 7b). All the other judgements he has mentioned are also intended to serve as warnings.[20]

Conclusion

These three examples from past judgements show that God judges not only those who are in a covenant relationship with him (Israel), but also angels and Gentiles who disobey him. He is "the Judge of all the earth" (Gen 18:25), and everyone must answer to him. All the ungodly, whether inside or outside the church, will face God's judgement.

Questions for Discussion

1. Jude wrote to urge the church to fight to keep the faith pure. How do we recognize false teaching? (Consult Jude 4 and 1 John 2:18–25; 4:1–6?)

2. Are there any wrong teachings in your community today? If so, try to identify these teachings and explain why they are wrong.

3. What is the Christian way to respond to the false teaching you identified? How should you respond to it when it comes from people claiming to be Christians?

4. How should you respond when false teaching comes from people of other faiths?

IDENTIFYING INFILTRATORS

A few years ago a preacher claiming to be a man of God established a healing and deliverance ministry in a nearby town. Over the course of two years, he won many followers to whom he made all kinds of prophecies – including that if they gave him seed money, they would be blessed financially. Gradually it became apparent that his prophecies were not being fulfilled, and his congregation began to shrink. People began to complain about him. One night he secretly packed his bags and fled, taking the church's money with him. No one has heard of him since. He may well have established a similar ministry in a different town. Fraudulent preachers like this bring the whole church into disrepute and destroy the faith of many.

In hindsight, it is easy to see signs that should have alerted people to the fact that he was a fraud. But how can we stop people from being deluded in the first place? The way to do this is by making sure that people know the warning signs – many of which Jude outlines in this part of his letter. People who know the difference between true Christian character and that of fraudsters will not be deceived. Jude equips us with such knowledge.

Verses 8–16 The Sins of the Infiltrators

Jude has already given us some general ideas about the ways in which the people who had infiltrated the church were sinning. Before getting into the details of their sins, he makes one other telling point. These people trust *their dreams* more than they trust the word of the Lord (v. 8a). They are not alone in this. There are many today who claim to have revelations from the Lord through dreams and visions. I know a woman who often argues with her pastor, even though he faithfully preaches the word of God. She is not as interested in what the Bible says as in words of prophecy based on dreams and visions. She thus rejects the authority of God's word and the pastor God has placed over her. Sadly, her attitude is common in Africa.

It is not that God never speaks in dreams. The Scriptures speak of God-given dreams (Joel 2:28). But they also warn that false prophets tend to rely heavily on dreams and prophetic lies (Isa 56:10; Jer 23:25, 26; 27:9; 29:8). We need to learn to discern which dreams come from God, and which from other sources. One test is that dreams that are not in keeping with God's character and the words of Scripture do not come from God. The dreams of the people against whom Jude is warning his readers fail this test because they direct people into paths of sins.

***Polluting their own bodies* (v. 8b).** The term translated "polluting" occurs five times in the New Testament and can carry overtones of ritual impurity (see John 18:28). This pollution can arise from roots of bitterness (Heb 12:15). The term is paired with unbelief in Titus 1:5: "to those who are corrupted and do not believe, nothing is pure. In fact, both their minds and consciences are corrupted". In the context of Jude, the term refers to immoral behaviour stemming from lack of faith in the Sovereign Lord Jesus. That Jude links the pollution to the flesh suggests that sexual immorality may be in view, indicating that the false teachers were sexually immoral. Paul, in warning believers, links sexual immorality to the defiling of the body as well: "Flee from sexual immorality. All other sins a person commits are outside the body, but whoever sins sexually, sins against their own body" (1 Cor 6:18). He also told the Corinthians to "honour God with your bodies" (1 Cor 6:20). Those who try to explain away God's commands on the basis that they have had some vision that exempts them from obeying his word will necessarily defile their bodies, often through sexual immorality.

There are some who claim that the pollution Jude is talking about comes from sexual dreams, or as J. B. Phillips translates it, "sexual fantasies". If so, he is not speaking about the sort of dreams that sometimes come unbidden in our sleep but about the sort of dreams that we encourage by watching pornography. These days, there are many who excuse such behaviour, saying that "everyone watches it". But it should not be so among those who heed Jesus' warning that "anyone who looks at a woman lustfully has already committed adultery with her in his heart" (Matt 5:28). Sanctification happens where the truth of God's word is cherished, for it revives us, makes us wise, rejoices our hearts, enlightens our eyes, and guards us from sin (Ps 19:7–8; 119:11).

Rejecting authority (v. 8c). Those who rely solely on dreams for guidance reject the authority of God's word. This same group also reject Jesus, who has absolute authority over all things (v. 4). They are unwilling to submit their dreams to the test of Scripture, the word of Christ. Once they have rejected the authority of Jesus and of God's word, it is a small step to reject all other authorities as well.

This is something we need to be aware of as new ministries spring up everywhere. Sometimes, these ministries are needed and their leaders are led by God. But it is a danger sign when someone wants to establish a new ministry because he or she hates being under any authority and rejects the supervision of godly leaders or religious bodies. Where there is a spirit of rebellion, there is a strong possibility that the leader may be led by dreams and fantasies rather than by the word of God.

Heaping abuse on celestial beings (v. 8d). The word translated *heap abuse* is also translated as "blaspheme" (ESV), "revile" (NASB, RSV), "speak evil of" (KJV) or "slander" (NRSV). We do not know what exactly these people were saying, but clearly it was extremely insulting. But who were they insulting? Here too we have a wealth of translations "dignities" (KJV), "the glorious ones" (ESV) and "angelic majesties" (NASB). Who are these beings? The term used is the Greek equivalent of a Hebrew expression that can refer simply to famous people (see Ps 149:8; Isa 3:5; 23:8), but it is never used with that meaning in Greek. It seems more likely that the beings referred to here are angels.[21] But are they holy angels or fallen angels? From the example that Jude gives in verse 9, it seems likely that they were evil angels. But should one not speak evil of fallen angels? Why it is wrong to do so?

From the context, it seems that what was happening was that the people who had infiltrated the church were so full of pride that, like the angels in verse 6, they forgot their place and overstepped their authority. They may have been claiming that demons had no power to hurt them,[22] or that they had the right to tell spiritual beings what to do, or the authority to mock spiritual beings and constrain their power. There are many African traditional healers who have claimed similar powers. Unfortunately, there are some Christian leaders who make similar claims. They would be wise to heed the example of the Archangel Michael, who did not insult Satan or *condemn him for slander but said, "The Lord rebuke you!"* (v. 9). He did not take the authority upon himself to judge Satan but surrendered to the Lord who has all authority in heaven and on earth. If even the most powerful archangel does not have the audacity to heap abuse on a spiritual being, how much more careful should we be.

In this reference to a dispute between an archangel and the devil, Jude is not referring to the Old Testament, for the account of the death of Moses in Deuteronomy 34 never refers to the devil or to Michael or to any dispute over the body of Moses.[23] Many scholars think that Jude is actually referring to a story from an apocryphal work called the *Assumption of Moses*.[24] This comes as a surprise to some, and may prompt them to ask how Jude can cite a source that is not part of Scripture. Yet Paul does the same in Acts 17:28 and Titus 1:12 where he quotes Greek and Cretan poets. Both Jude and Paul were referring to things that were familiar to their readers to help them understand a point they were making. In other words, they were using sermon illustrations. They were not claiming that these other writing were divinely inspired like the Scriptures.

The words ascribed to the archangel Michael, *The Lord rebuke you!* are, however, found in the Old Testament. They are found in Zechariah 3:2, where God rebukes Satan and vindicates Joshua the high priest.

The people Jude was condemning were claiming to have such knowledge of the spiritual realm that they could even abuse spiritual beings. In reality, they were putting themselves in danger by speaking about things they did *not understand* (v. 10a). God does not excuse those who refuse to acquire knowledge and prefer to rely on their sinful instincts (Isa 5:13; Hos 4:6; Prov 1:29).

Jude warns that those who rely on their instincts will be destroyed by those instincts (v. 10b). He compares them to unreasoning animals – like Nebuchadnezzar, whose mind was changed from man's to a beast's, so that he ate grass like an ox (Dan 4:16, 32).

Verse 11 The Role Models for the Infiltrators

Young people starting out in life are often advised to choose someone as a role model. Unfortunately, the role models many young people choose are corrupt politicians, unethical business people, or celebrities who love to flash their wealth around and boast of a lifestyle that does not honour God. Nevertheless, many imitate them. Often, this imitation is subconscious – you only become aware of the significant influence a model has had on you when you find yourself acting, speaking, and gesturing the way they do.

It seems that the infiltrators in the church also had role models. But they had chosen very poorly. Jude points out that their models were three evil men from the Old Testament: Cain, Balaam, and Korah. The consequences of their poor choices are summed up in the words, *Woe to them!* (v. 11a; see also Isa 3:11; 5:8, 20; Nah 3:1; Matt 23). Their behaviour is bringing a curse on them and they will know misery.[25]

Cain murdered his brother, and so God placed a curse on him, just as he had placed a curse on the serpent in Eden (Gen 3:14; 4:1–11). The Apostle John has this to say about Cain: "We should not be like Cain, who was of the evil one and murdered his brother. And why did he murder him? Because his own deeds were evil and his brother's righteous" (1 John 3:12 ESV). Like Cain, the infiltrators reject God's authority and engage in destructive behaviour that will destroy their souls and those of others.[26] So when we contend for the faith, we are fighting to prevent the spiritual equivalent of murder or fratricide.

Balaam was a prophet who saw prophecy as a path to wealth (Num 22–24; Neh 13:2), practised divination (Josh 13:22), and advised the Moabites to lure the Israelites into Baal worship (Num 31:16; see also

25:1–3).[27] Just as Balaam prophesied for selfish gain and sought to lure Israel away from God, so the infiltrators in Jude's day were more interested in *profit* and satisfying their own lust than in serving God and the church.

Korah was a man who started a rebellion against the authority of Moses and Aaron, which ended very badly for him and his household (Num 16). Like him, the infiltrators were refusing to accept the authority of the apostles and of God's word and denying even the authority of Christ (v. 4). Their immoral lifestyle, disregard for God's word, and denial of Jesus' lordship are all signs of the rebellion that will result in their eternal destruction (v. 11c). In fact, their destruction is so certain that Jude can even speak of it using the past tense (*they have been destroyed*).[28]

Verses 12–13 Metaphors That Describe the Infiltrators

Jude next uses seven vivid images to describe the negative influence of the infiltrators.

They are blemishes at your love feasts (v. 12a).[29] *Love feasts* were the gatherings of believers in the early church to eat and observe the Lord's Supper (see also 1 Cor 11:27–32). But these infiltrators stain and discolour the religious feasts of the saints (see my commentary on 2 Pet 2:13). They disguise themselves as angels of light, but they are nothing of the kind (see 2 Cor 11:12–14). It is not enough to be part of the fellowship meal of believers; we must evaluate whether we are influencing the community for good or for ill.

They eat with you without the slightest qualm (v. 12b). The words *with you* show that these people blend in with God's people, feasting without any fear of judgement. They ignore Paul's warning that "everyone ought to examine themselves" before partaking of the Lord's Supper because failure to do so will bring God's judgement (1 Cor 11:27–32). These infiltrators happily share in the Lord's Supper even as they deny him (v. 4). Sadly, there are still people like that today. Some people offer a sacrifice in accordance with African Traditional Religion one day and come to the communion table on the next. The Lord's table is reserved only for those who honour Christ alone as Lord.

They are shepherds who feed only themselves (v. 12c). The fact that Jude refers to these people as *shepherds* suggests that some of these infiltrators may have attained leadership positions within the church (see Acts 20:28). They were greedy shepherds, like those described by the prophet Ezekiel (Ezek 34:2–5, 8, 10). Their goal was not to care for the flock but to satisfy their own desires. Getting what they wanted was more important to them than the needs of the flock (see John 10:12–13). The prosperity preachers today who amass wealth for themselves at the expense of their poor followers are not different from the false teachers Jude describes. They see the ministry as a means of enriching themselves.

They are clouds without rain, blown along by the wind (v. 12d). In a time of drought, the sight of clouds stirs hope that there will be rain at last. Disappointment sets in when the wind scatters the clouds. Similarly, the infiltrators attract hopeful attention, for they promise much. But those who look to them with hope are invariably disappointed, for these people have nothing to give (Prov 25:14; see also 2 Pet 2:17). They are like false preachers today who promise wealth and health but never grant them. They promise to refresh the people, but they cannot do so since they themselves are cut off from Jesus, the sole source of refreshing water (John 4:10).

They are autumn trees, without fruit and uprooted – twice dead (v. 12e). The infiltrators are like trees that have no fruit in the harvest season (autumn). Fruitless trees are as good as dead, and when they are finally uprooted they are literally dead, so then they are *twice dead* or completely useless.[30] Jude has no doubt that these false teachers will be seen in their true colours when the harvest time comes. Having borne no fruit of righteousness, they will be uprooted (see also Matt 15:13). To put it another way, they are already "dead in their trespasses and sins" (Eph 2:1) and will also die the second death of eternal condemnation (Rev 2:11; 21:8).

They are wild waves of the sea, foaming up their shame (v. 13a). Thinking about the behaviour of these men reminds Jude of Isaiah's words: "The wicked are like the tossing sea, for it cannot be quiet, and its waters toss up mire and dirt" (Isa 57:20 ESV). Like the waves of the sea, these people are restless and uncontrolled. Just as the waves of the sea spread debris on the beach, so these people spread moral filth, their *shame*. Unlike true believers who spread the fragrance of Christ, these people make others ungodly wherever they go.

They are wandering stars (v. 13b). We sometimes think of a "wandering star" as a planet, but that is not how Jude is using this image here. He may be thinking of these people as being like the stars whose fall is a sign of God's judgement (Matt 24:29; Mark 13:25; Rev 6:13). Or he may be using this image in the same way that John does in the book of Revelation, where stars represent church leaders (Rev 1:16, 20–2:1; 2:28; 3:1). Unlike the star that led the wise men from the east to Jesus (Matt 2:2), these leaders lead people away from him. No one should look to them for direction and spiritual guidance because they are utterly unreliable.

Jude concludes this list of metaphors with the words, *for whom blackest darkness has been reserved forever* (v. 13c). Just as a shooting star plunges into the dark, so these wandering stars are extinguished. These fruitless, restless, lawless people will experience the *blackest darkness* that God has reserved for them.[31] This is the same darkness to which God consigned the angels who sinned and the false teachers whom Peter condemned (v. 6; 2 Pet 2:4, 17). This darkness may be like that which God brought upon Egypt when he judged that nation for its oppression of his people (Exod 10:21–22), but it is eternal. Eternal judgement awaits all those who bring blemishes on God's people.

Verses 14–16 A Prophecy against the Infiltrators

Jude uses a quotation to reinforce his point about the future of the ungodly intruders. Before looking at the quotation, it may be helpful to look at its source. It comes from a book that was probably written during the first century BC and was popular among first-century Jews. Jude identifies it by its supposed author, *Enoch, the seventh from Adam* (v. 14).[32]

The fact that Jude quotes a prophecy from this book does not mean that he is asserting that it is divinely inspired or has the same authority as Scripture.[33] As before (see on v. 9), he is doing what other biblical writers sometimes do when they quote from the literature of their time to illustrate a point they are making. Paul, for example, quoted Greek poets (Acts 17:28; 1 Cor 15:33) and a Cretan prophet (Titus 1:12). While the works cited were not originally inspired in the same way as the Scriptures are, the passages quoted are now part of Scriptures and are inspired to serve the purpose for which they were cited. It is also worth noting that the prophecy that Jude cites from the book of *Enoch* is very similar to other prophecies in Scriptures.

The *Enoch* whose name is attached to the prophecy in verses 14–15 was the seventh from Adam in the sense that in the genealogical lists in Genesis 5:1–24 and 1 Chronicles 1:1–3 he appears in the seventh generation after Adam. He was revered as a man who walked closely with the Lord (Gen 5:22–24; see also Heb 11:5), which is most likely why the anonymous author of the book of Enoch chose to adopt his name.

The prophecy that Jude cites is that the Lord will come with his angels to judge people for their *ungodly acts* and *the defiant words ungodly sinners have spoken against him* (v. 14–15). This is an accurate description of the sins and judgement of the infiltrators, and it is also a recurrent theme in both the Old and New Testaments (see Isa 66:15–16; Jer 25:31; Zech 14:5; Mal 3:5; Matt 16:27; 25:31–33; 2 Thess 1:7–8).

Verse 16 Final Description of the Infiltrators

Jude concludes his description of the infiltrators by mentioning five characteristics which show that they are indeed wicked and that Enoch's prophesy of judgement, which accords with Old and New Testament prophecies, applies to them.

They are grumblers. Like the Israelites who grumbled against God and were destroyed (Exod 16:7; Num 14:29; 1 Cor 10:10), these men grumble against God because they want to follow their own desires. True believers are called to a generous and cheerful service of God and each other without grumbling (Phil 2:14; Jas 5:9; 1 Pet 4:9).

They are faultfinders. The translation *faultfinders* stresses that they are chronic complainers. But we get a slightly different perspective when we notice that this word can also be translated "malcontents" (ESV, RSV) and "discontented" (HCSB[34]). They are the type of people who are never satisfied with what they have but have an insatiable craving for more. They cannot understand what Paul means when he says that "godliness with contentment is great gain" (1 Tim 6:6–7 ESV). Instead, they are among those who use godliness as "a means to financial gain" (1 Tim 6:5) and remain unsatisfied until they get what they want.

They follow their own evil desires. The apostles had warned believers that scoffers would come following their own desires (v. 18; see also 2 Pet 3:3), and the infiltrators are exactly the types of people they had in mind. The false teachers are not interested in walking in God's way but only in doing what they want (see also Jer 18:12; Isa 65:2; 2 Tim 4:3). By contrast, true believers live to serve God, not themselves (1 Pet 4:2).

They boast about themselves. Literally, "their mouths speak boastful words". These people are eager to talk about how wonderful and successful they are in an attempt to impress others and attract followers (see also 2 Pet 2:18). They are more interested in how other people see them than in how God sees them – which is far more important (see John 5:44; 12:26, 43; Rom 2:29). We still see false teachers whose main aim is to impress and attract crowds by boasting about their power and the people they know.

It is also possible that their "boastful words" are an expression of "their arrogant, presumptuous attitude towards God, their insolent contempt for his commandments, their rejection of his moral authority which amounts to a proud claim to be their own moral authority."[35]

They flatter others for their own advantage. The word rendered *flatter* is best translated "show partiality" (compare Lev 19:15; Deut 10:17; 2 Chr 19:7; Prov 18:5; Job 32:21; 34:19).[36] Those who undermine the church treat people differently; the rich receive special attention while the poor are ignored, and even treated badly. But those who fear God are expected to be free from partiality, for all those whom Christ has redeemed have equal standing before God and should be treated equally (Jas 2:1–9; also Job 34:19; Gal 3:28).

This is a sin that it is easy for all of us to fall into. To give only one example, we may treat a Westerner with greater respect than we show to our African sisters and brothers, or assume that a book by a Western writer is somehow better than one by an African writer. That too is wrong, and it too deserves God's judgement. While we are commanded to give honour to those whom honour is due (Rom 13:7), this should never be done in way that humiliate others.

Questions for Discussion

1. In what ways are the prosperity preachers in Africa similar or dissimilar to the people Jude describes and condemns?

2. Are you ever tempted by some of the sins Jude mentions? For example, do you sometimes want to grumble, or to exaggerate a little in order to impress people? If so, how do you resist these temptations?

3. Would you consider yourself someone who truly belongs to the community of God's people or are you an infiltrator? Do you see some of the attitudes Jude describes in your own life? If so, repent of these attitudes and ask your brothers and sisters in the Lord to pray that God will deliver you from them.

PERSEVERE IN THE FAITH

At the start of every flight on an airplane, the cabin crew explains the safety procedures in case of an emergency on the flight. These include telling you that if there is a problem with the air pressure in the cabin, oxygen masks will drop from the ceiling. They show you how to put on the mask if you need it, and then they always add, "If you are travelling with a child, put on your own mask before you put the mask on the child". Why? Surely a mother or father would put their child's need for air above their own. But the cabin crew have a good reason for this apparently selfish order – you as the parent need to have the oxygen first so that you can think clearly and do what is needed to save your child, including carrying him or her out of the plane if that becomes necessary. So you put on your oxygen mask first in order to be able to save your child.

Jude's instructions to the church are somewhat similar to those given on the plane. Believers are to make sure that they stay true to the holy faith, because only then will they be able to save others who are wavering because of the false teaching they are hearing from infiltrators.

Verses 17–19 Remember the Words of the Apostles

Once again Jude addresses his audience as his *dear friends* (v. 17a; see comment on v. 3). He does not want them to feel that his anger at the infiltrators is directed at them. What he does want to do is to remind them that the presence of such people is not something that should surprise them. The apostles had known that such people would come and had warned that *in the last times there will be scoffers* (v. 18a; see Acts 20:29–30; 1 Tim 4:1–5; 2 Tim 3:1–5).[37]

The *last times* is an expression that refers to the whole period between Christ's first coming and his second coming (Heb 1:2; see also Acts 2:17; 1 Pet 1:20). It includes both Jude's day and our day. So it is not surprising that we too encounter false teachers who prefer to *follow their own ungodly desires* rather than obeying God (v. 18b).

Like those to whom Jude was writing, we need to *remember what the apostles of our Lord Jesus Christ foretold* (v. 17b). To *remember* in this context is not merely to recall a fact but to have that fact imprinted on our hearts and minds, and to let it guide our conduct. This is particularly important when it comes to the apostles' teaching, for it is the foundation on which the church stands (see Eph 2:20; 1 Cor 15:1–11).

The infiltrators do not unite people around the apostolic teaching. Instead, they *divide* them by introducing ideas and behaviour that are contrary to that teaching and so lead to arguments within the church (v. 19a). Such divisions are harmful. So are divisions based on external categories like race, ethnicity, wealth, or social class. The church is called to stand united, and we must be on guard against those who sow division (see also Rom 16:17; 1 Cor 12:12–14).

The teaching of the apostles is rooted in the teaching of our Lord Jesus Christ and in the word of God, but the teaching of the infiltrators is rooted in *mere natural instinct* (v. 19b). Anyone who thinks like this "does not accept the things that come from the Spirit of God but considers them foolishness, and cannot understand them because they are discerned only through the Spirit" (1 Cor 2:14). James' words about demonic and earthly wisdom would describe the instincts of the false teachers: "If you harbour bitter envy and selfish ambition in your hearts, do not boast about it or deny the truth. Such 'wisdom' does not come down from heaven but is earthly, unspiritual, demonic" (Jas 3:14–15).

People who favour earthly and demonic wisdom are not true believers in Jesus Christ. So we are not surprised to hear Jude say that they *do not have the Spirit* (v. 19c) who is given to all who are truly saved (Rom 8:9; 1 Cor 3:16). Even though the false teachers take part in the activities of the church, even sharing in the love feasts (v. 12), they are not part of Christ's church. The Spirit of Christ does not indwell them.

Verses 20–21 Keep Yourselves in God's Love

Yet again Jude addresses his readers as his *dear friends* as he urges them saying, *keep yourselves in God's love* (v. 21). The phrase *God's love* could refer to the love we have for God or the love God has for us.[38] The former is the love that is explicitly commanded in both the Old and New Testaments (Deut 6:5; 10:12; Josh 22:5; Matt 22:37; Mark 12:30; Luke 10:27). The latter is the way Jude described the believers at the start of this letter (vv. 1–2). While the first option seems the most likely in this context,[39] to focus on the issue of which interpretation is correct is to miss the larger question of how Jude can command us to keep ourselves in God's love, whether his love for us or our love for him. In pondering this question, we need to remember that as Christians we are not called to "let go and let God" as the saying goes. Jude has already called on us to contend for the faith, and now he calls on us to cling to God's love.

Jude 20–21 uses three participle clauses to describe the way to keep ourselves in God's love. These clauses, *building yourselves up in your most holy faith, praying in the Holy Spirit*, and *waiting for the mercy of our Lord Jesus Christ*, all modify the main clause, *keep yourselves in God's love*.[40]

The first of these clauses say that we keep ourselves in God's love by *building [ourselves] up in [our] most holy faith* (v. 20a). "The most holy faith" is the body of truth, the teaching of the apostles (Rom 6:17; 1 Cor 15:3). So one way we keep ourselves in the love of God, whether our love for him or his for us, is by feeding our souls with God's word, the teaching enshrined in the Scriptures. When we neglect the Scriptures, we are being negligent about preserving ourselves in God's love. Like the early church we are to devote ourselves to learning and being taught the word of God (Acts 2:42). Writing to the Christians in Colossae, Paul gave them the same encouragement: "Let the message of Christ dwell among you richly as you teach and admonish one another with all wisdom, through psalms, hymns and songs from the Spirit, singing to God with gratitude in your hearts" (Col 3:16).

The second way we keep ourselves in God's love is by *praying in the Holy Spirit*. Jude is not saying that we need to speak in tongues when we pray, for not all believers have the gift of tongues (1 Cor 12:30). But all of us who have God's Spirit can obey this command by praying in the power of the Holy Spirit, with our prayers informed by the Holy Spirit-inspired Scriptures so that they are in accordance with the will of the Spirit (Rom 8:26–27; Eph 6:18). This is something the infiltrators cannot do because they lack the Spirit (v. 19). As we communicate with God in prayer and express our dependence on him, we are kept in his love.

The third way we keep ourselves in God's love is by waiting *for the mercy of our Lord Jesus Christ to bring you to eternal life* (v. 21).[41] We are to wait expectantly for Christ's return when we will fully enjoy the life we enjoy in part in the present. To wait for something is to look forward to it with eager expectation. Eager longing for Christ's return will guard us from straying from the love of God.

Jude's reference to *the mercy of the Lord Jesus Christ* that will lead us into eternal life reminds us that our salvation – past, present and future – is based solely on the mercy of Christ. We do nothing to earn it. None of us has any grounds for boasting that we somehow deserve to be saved. In fact, all the means for preserving ourselves in God's love are supplied by God: the word of God, the Spirit who helps us pray, and the mercy of God in Christ. This link to all three persons of the Trinity in verses 21–22 shows that the entire Godhead is involved in the miracle of our perseverance in the love of God.

Jude began this letter by reminding his readers that they are being kept by God for Jesus Christ (v. 1), and the letter ends on the same reassuring note (v. 24). If that is the case, how does our keeping of ourselves in God's love relate to God's keeping of us? Given the Trinitarian involvement we noted in the previous verse, and the fact that the letter is enveloped by God's keeping of the believers, we can surmise that believers only keep themselves in God's love because God is keeping them. Without God's preserving grace, we cannot build ourselves in the most holy faith, pray in the Spirit, or wait for future mercy.

We can obey the command to keep ourselves in God's love because God has already loved us. He has displayed his love for us in the death of Christ (Rom 5:8; see also 1 John 4:9–10) and shown us mercy (Eph 2:4). His Spirit has poured God's love into our hearts so that we can love God as we ought to (Rom 5:5; see also 2 Thess 3:5). Thus ultimately it is God who enables us to love him and to keep ourselves in his love.

In the Old Testament Israel failed to love God because their hearts were uncircumcised (Deut 29:4). But God promised that the day would come when he would circumcise his people's hearts so that they would love him completely (Deut 30:6). That day came with the coming of Christ (Col 2:11) and so now he has indeed enabled us to love him. Thus we must guard our hearts from falling in love with other objects. God alone must be the sole object of all our affections.

Our love for God is the wellspring of our obedience to God (John 14:15, 21, 23–24; 1 John 2:5; 5:3). The Old Testament makes it clear that those who love God obey God (Exod 20:6; Deut 5:10; 7:9; 11:1; 19:9; 30:16; Josh 22:5; Dan 9:4). Jesus, too, told us that we abide in God's (Jesus') love by obeying his commands (John 15:9–11). So we will know whether or not we are keeping ourselves in God's love by what we do with God's commands. Obedience to his commands indicates that we are keeping ourselves in his love, but disobedience shows that our heart is accepting and loving someone or something other than God.

In 1 Corinthians 13:3 Paul speaks of faith, hope, and love and argues that the highest of these virtues is love. Based on Paul exaltation of love, we conclude that we are to build ourselves up in *faith* (v. 20a), fix our gaze on the hope of Christ's mercy (v. 21b), and so persevere in the highest virtue, *love* (v. 21a).[42]

To sum up what has been said, God draws our hearts to his love (2 Thess 3:5), and we must keep ourselves in his love by building ourselves up in the holy faith, praying in the Spirit, and waiting for Christ's mercy that will bring us into eternal joy.

Verses 22–23 Show Mercy

After encouraging the true believers to stand firm in God's love, Jude turns to the question of how they are to respond to those who have been influenced by the infiltrators, with some beginning to doubt what they have been taught, others teetering on the verge of eternal judgement, and others already completely corrupted.[43] The believers need to approach these three groups in different ways.

When it comes to those who are now troubled by doubt, Jude commands the church to *be merciful* (v. 22). The church should not reject those who are questioning doctrines they once embraced. Instead, the church should gently correct them, in hope that God will restore them to a secure faith (see 2 Tim 2:25). By doing this, they may save doubters from spiritual death (Jas 5:19–20; see also 1 John 5:16–18).

Others have advanced so far into doubt that they are now on the verge of disbelief and in great risk of falling into eternal judgement (v. 23). These people may have accepted the infiltrators' arguments and are beginning to adopt their way of life. The church is called to save those who were in such danger by *snatching them from the fire* (v. 23). We could think of this in terms of a mother who rushes into a burning home to save her child, even if she herself may suffer terrible burns in the process. But whereas she rescues her child from physical fire, the church is to rescue these endangered believers from the eternal fire of God's judgement (see Matt 3:10, 12; 5:22; Mark 9:43, 48; Heb 10:27; Rev 19:20; 20:10, 14, 15; 21:8). Our response to seeing someone in such danger should not be any less urgent than that of a mother who acts to save her child.

Jude's Jewish readers would have recognized an Old Testament allusion in this image. After the Jews returned from exile in Babylon, the prophet Zechariah had a vision in which he saw Satan accusing the high priest of being unworthy of his position. Satan's accusation may have been true, for Joshua was "dressed in filthy clothes", which were unworthy of his office. But the Lord himself rebuked Satan and described Joshua as "a burning stick snatched from the fire". Then an angel removed Joshua's filthy clothes, cleansed him of sin, and gave him priestly robes and priestly authority (Zech 3:1–6; see also Amos 4:11). This is what Jude wants the church to do for those who are falling into sin. They are to be brought back and restored to fellowship.

Jude does not say exactly how the church is go about doing this. The approach may vary from person to person. However, the verb "snatch" indicates determined action, not mere passive wishing that someone will return to the faith.[44] The action should not be violent – there is no justification here for beating, abducting or imprisoning people if they are considering leaving the faith. What Jude is calling for is a deliberate, determined effort to rescue those who are at the verge of eternal destruction.

Finally, there are those who have already been morally corrupted by the infiltrators. Jude commands the church to show mercy to such people too (v. 23). They are not to be subjected to public derision and hatred. The believers' mercy must, however, be *mixed with fear*, for there is a real danger that they themselves will be drawn into sin (see Gal 6:1; 1 Cor 4:21). The restoration process must also be associated with a very real hatred for the filthy garments of sin (Zech 3:3–4, see also 2 Cor 7:1; Rev 3:4).

Questions for Discussion

1. How would you approach someone in your church who is in danger of falling away from the faith, or who has left the faith? After formulating your answer, consult Galatians 6:1; 2 Timothy 2:25; 1 Peter 4:8; and 2 Thessalonians 3:15. Do these verses prompt you to modify your earlier answer in any way?

2. In verse 20, Jude talks about praying in the Holy Spirit. What does this mean in this context? See also Ephesians 6:18 and Romans 8:26.

3. In what practical ways can you keep yourself in the love of God?

RESCUING FROM THE FIRE

Jude's command to snatch those who are in danger from the fire reminds me of what was done for a Christian brother who was swimming in an ocean of sexual sin, lust and pornography. Whenever God convicted him of his sin, he would vow that it would stop and would live in light of that commitment for a few days. But all too soon he would again be drowning in the same ocean.

No one in his church was aware of what was going on. This brother acted righteous before others. He pretended he was zealous. He would even preach and teach. But gradually God in his mercy caused others within his congregation to start observing that something was wrong with this brother. They began to pray for him, pleading with God that he would convict their erring brother of his sin, give him godly sorrow, and enable him to repent.

While the other leaders were on their knees, one of them set out to confront the brother about his sin. Things did not go well the first few times they met. He adamantly rejected any suggestion that he was living in sin. So the leaders continued to pray, and God heard and answered their prayers.

The day came when this brother could no longer hide his sin because the burden of pretence was killing him. He felt like David in Psalm 32:3–4 "When I kept silent, my bones wasted away through my groaning all day long. For day and night your hand was heavy on me; my strength was sapped as in the heat of summer" (NIV). His own hypocrisy became increasingly unbearable to him. He mustered the courage by help of the Holy Spirit and confessed his sin, just as David does in Psalm 32:5: "I acknowledged my sin to you and did not cover up my iniquity; I said 'I will confess my transgressions to the LORD,' and you forgave the iniquity of my sin" (ESV).

When this brother confessed his sin to the brother who had confronted him, the elders prayerfully and gently rebuked him and ensured that his repentance was genuine, giving him time to show evidence of the change. After a period of time, they restored him to full communion with the body. He now shares sweet fellowship with God's people, striving side-by-side his brothers and sisters for the faith. He wants to be used by God to instruct those who desire to walk in the path that he walked

Things ended well with this brother, for he repented and was restored into fellowship. That does always happen. But the church must not give up pursuing and praying for those who are erring, correcting those who oppose the gospel by their lifestyle with gentleness. We must do this "in hope that God will grant them repentance leading them to a knowledge of the truth, and that they will come to their senses and escape from the trap of the devil, who has taken them captive to do his will" (2 Tim 2:25–26 NIV).

Are there brothers or sisters around you who are living in sin, and as a result, showing that they are on the path to hell? Does the story above give you any idea about how you could set about rescuing them? In what way should your church and its leaders be involved in this process?

CONCLUDING DOXOLOGY

In African Traditional Religion, people pray to many divinities and spirits. They may ask for things such as a good harvest or for rain. A woman may pray to a specific idol if she has trouble conceiving a child. When trouble strikes, people turn to the spirits to find out whether they have offended the ancestors or one of the tribal gods and then do something to placate them. Even some who claim to be Christian offer sacrifices to and honour these idols and spirits. But the Bible is clear that there is only one God, and that he controls the world and our individual destiny. He is the only one who is worthy to be worshipped for who he is, what he has done, and what he will do. Jude reminds us of this as he closes his letter with a great doxology, or hymn of praise to God.

Jude's words here are often used as a blessing at the end of worship services, and may be so familiar to us that we have ceased to think about them. It is good to pause and reflect on them so that we can add our "Amen" from full and thankful hearts.

Verse 24 Praise for What God Does

Jude begins his doxology by praising God for what he is able to do for his people (see also Rom 16:25; Eph 3:20). In the context of this letter, the point that is highest in Jude's mind is that God is able to keep his people *from stumbling* (v. 24a). This does not mean that we are flawless, since "we all stumble in many ways" (Jas 3:2; see also 1 Kgs 8:46; 1 John 1:8). Rather, it means that we will never stumble so badly that we will irreversibly fall into condemnation (see v. 23a). God will ultimately keep us secure in him so that we will not give up the faith (see also John 17:12; Phil 2:13; 2 Tim 1:12; 2 Thess 3:3). He has the power to do this.

The knowledge that God will keep us from stumbling does not mean that we can be careless about our faith and conduct – that is exactly the error that the infiltrators were making. We need to keep loving God and building ourselves up in the faith. But we can be confident that as we walk along the path of faith, and lay the bricks that build up our own characters and God's church, he will be there to catch us if we fall and prevent a fatal injury. For this we should praise him.

Jude's second reason for praising God flows from the first: he is also able *to present you before his glorious presence without fault and with great joy* (v. 24b). At the end of the age, God himself, who is now keeping believers faithful, will welcome them into his glorious presence with great joy.

The term translated *without fault* can also be rendered "blameless", "faultless" and "without blemish" (Eph 1:4; 5:27; Phil 2:15; Col 1:22). It represents the accomplishment of God plan, whereby he chose us "to be holy and blameless in his sight" (Eph 1:4).

In the Old Testament, worshippers were expected to bring an animal without any defect or fault to be sacrificed to atone for their sins (Lev 4:3; 5:15, 18; 6:6; 9:2–3; 12:6; Ezek 43:22–23; 45:18). Ultimately, Christ Jesus himself became the faultless sacrifice for our sins (Heb 9:14; 1 Pet 1:19). His perfect sacrifice accomplished far more than the sacrifice of animals, for it cleansed all our sin so that we too can be declared blameless in the sight of God (see Eph 5:27; Col 1:22; Rev 14:5). This was the mission for which Christ came to earth: "He [God] has reconciled you by Christ's physical body through death to present you holy in his sight, without blemish and free from accusation" (Col 1:22).

Christ's fulfilment of his mission is a source of great joy in heaven, as we know from John's vision of heavenly beings worshipping Jesus:

> You are worthy to take the scroll and to open its seals, because
> you were slain, and with your blood you purchased for God
> persons from every tribe and language and people and nation.

> You have made them to be a kingdom and priests to serve our
> God, and they will reign on the earth. (Rev 5:9–10)

It is no wonder then that there will be *great joy* when God's people are welcomed into his presence. When God presents us before him, not only will we rejoice in Christ's redeeming work that has made us faultless, but God himself will rejoice over us with *great joy*. God will take great delight in presenting his blood-bought people in the presence of his glory. And Jude is not the only one to say this. The prophet Zephaniah was told that God will take "great delight" in his redeemed people, and "will rejoice over you with singing" (Zeph 3:17; see also Isa 62:5; 65:19; Eph 1:4–5).

Verse 25 Praise for Who God Is

We do not only worship God for what he does, but also for who he is: *the only God* (v. 25a). The various gods worshipped in African Traditional Religion and in other world religions are not gods at all, as stated clearly in Psalm 96:5: "all the gods of the nations are idols, but the Lord [Yahweh] made the heavens".

There is only one true God. He is our Father (v. 1), the source of grace and love (vv. 1, 4, 21), and the only one worthy of eternal praise (Ps 96:4). Moses portrayed Israel's God as the only true God: "Hear O Israel: the Lord our God, the Lord is one" (Deut 6:4; see also Deut 6:39; 32:39; Isa 46:9; Jer 10:10; Joel 2:27). As the only God, he alone is worthy of eternal praise (Dan 2:20; Ps 41:13; Isa 48:11).

Jesus too stated that there is only one true God (John 5:44; 17:3). And the Apostle Paul honoured "the King eternal, immortal, invisible, the only God" (1 Tim 1:17; see also Rom 16:27; 1 Cor 8:4). This is the God Christian's worship. It is our prayer and aim that people everywhere will recognize that only this God deserves worship (v. 25).

Jude also identifies this one true God as *our Saviour* (v. 25b). God is often portrayed as the Saviour in the Old Testament. He saved Israel from Egypt, and continued to save his people (Pss 17:7; 106:21; Isa 43:3; 45:15, 21; 49:26; 60:16). In the New Testament, too, God is spoken of as a Saviour (Luke 1:47; 1 Tim 1:1; 2:3; 4:10; Titus 1:3; 2:10; 3:4), but the term *Saviour* is used much more often to describe Jesus, who initiated the new exodus that led us from slavery to sin into the freedom and glory of the children of God (Rom 8:21).[45]

Since Jesus and the Father are one (see, for example, John 10:30; 2 Pet 1:1), it is appropriate that both are given the title Saviour. Jesus and God the Father alone are worthy of praise as Saviour. No other deity can save from sin and death.

Verse 25b God Alone Is Worthy of Eternal Praise

Having described who God is and what he has accomplished for his people, Jude brings his doxology to an end on a high note declaring God worthy of *glory, majesty, power and authority* (v. 25b; see also Rom 16:27; Eph 3:21; 2 Pet 3:18).

"Glory signifies the honor, resplendence, and beauty that is ascribed to God for his saving work."[46] In the context of Jude's letter, God is worthy of glory because he has called us, loved us, and keeps us (vv. 1, 24).

The word *majesty* conveys a sense of God's awe-inspiring presence and greatness. Majesty is ascribed only to God the Father in the New Testament (Heb 1:3; 8:1). The Psalms too declare God's majesty: "Great is the LORD, and greatly to be praised, and his greatness is unsearchable" (Ps 145:3 ESV; see also Deut 32:3; Ps 150:2). Any majesty that we think is attached to anything or to any other being fades in comparison to God's majestic presence.

The last two words, *power* and *authority* are similar in meaning. Power refers to God's rule and sovereignty (see 1 Tim 6:16; 1 Pet 4:11; 5:11; Rev 1:6). God's authority is his absolute power and control over all things (Luke 12:5; Acts 1:7; Rom 9:21). He shares this authority with his Son (Matt 28:19–20). Jude says that it is *through Jesus Christ our Lord* that eternal glory, majesty, power, and authority are attributed to God (v. 25c; see also Rom 1:8; 16:27; 1 Pet 4:11).

The final phrase in Jude's doxology, *before all ages, now and forevermore* reminds us that God is eternally worthy of this praise (v. 25; see also Rom 16:27; Eph 3:21; 2 Pet 3:18). He always was, is now, and always will be the glorious, majestic, powerful, sovereign God. Believers should find comfort in the fact that our God is sovereign over all, Lord of lords and King of kings.

We should join Jude in saying *Amen*, affirming that our God is indeed who Jude says he is.

Questions for Discussion

1. What element in this letter has spoken to you most personally? How is it related to God's character? Can you lead the group in praising him for that attribute specifically?

2. Think about the fact that you will be brought into the presence of God "with great joy". What does that mean for your life today?

3. How would you explain to idol worshippers in your community that there is only one true God?

PARALLELS BETWEEN JUDE AND 2 PETER

In these commentaries I have not devoted much space to the similarities between Jude and 2 Peter, but here is a table of some of the major parallels. Jude and 2 Peter show many similarities as regards style, language, argument, themes, order of material, and illustrations. It is possible that one of the authors drew on the other or that they both got their material from the same source. Some argue that Jude made use of 2 Peter,[47] while most scholars argue that 2 Peter used Jude. It seems that the latter is the most probable position for several reasons: first, Jude is shorter than 2 Peter, which makes it most likely that Peter used Jude and expanded on this material. Second, we see that Jude speaks much more harshly than Peter does, suggesting that the content of Jude was toned down in 2 Peter. Third, Jude makes use of apocryphal books but 2 Peter does not, suggesting that Peter avoided them because of their unorthodox nature.[48]

For the above reasons, and others listed by Donald Guthrie, I think that the author of 2 Peter drew on Jude.[49] One must, however, hold loosely to any conclusion on this matter because there is no definitive proof. Even Guthrie is uncertain in his conclusion about which author wrote first. Fortunately, this question does not affect the way we interpret these books. Both are inspired and helpful for instructing us in the faith, and each must be studied in its own right, which is the approached I have taken in these commentaries.

Similar Content

	2 Peter		Jude
2:1–3	But there were also false prophets among the people, just as there will be false teachers among you. They will secretly introduce destructive heresies, even denying the sovereign Lord who bought them–bringing swift destruction on themselves. Many will follow their depraved conduct and will bring the way of truth into disrepute. In their greed these teachers will exploit you with fabricated stories. Their condemnation has long been hanging over them, and their destruction has not been sleeping.	4	For certain individuals whose condemnation was written about long ago have secretly slipped in among you. They are ungodly people, who pervert the grace of our God into a license for immorality and deny Jesus Christ our only Sovereign and Lord.
2:4	For if God did not spare angels when they sinned, but sent them to hell, putting them in chains of darkness to be held for judgement	6	And the angels who did not keep their positions of authority but abandoned their proper dwelling–these he has kept in darkness, bound with everlasting chains for judgement on the great Day.
2:6	If he condemned the cities of Sodom and Gomorrah by burning them to ashes, and made them an example of what is going to happen to the ungodly	7	In a similar way, Sodom and Gomorrah and the surrounding towns gave themselves up to sexual immorality and perversion. They serve as an example of those who suffer the punishment of eternal fire
2:10	This is especially true of those who follow the corrupt desire of the sinful nature and despise authority. Bold and arrogant, they are not afraid to heap abuse on celestial beings	8	In the very same way, on the strength of their dreams these ungodly people pollute their own bodies, reject authority and heap abuse on celestial beings.
2:11	Yet even angels, although they are stronger and more powerful, do not heap abuse on such beings when bringing judgement on them from the Lord.	9	But even the archangel Michael, when he was disputing with the devil about the body of Moses, did not himself dare to condemn him for slander but said, "The Lord rebuke you!"

2:12	But these people blaspheme in matters they do not understand. They are like unreasoning animals, creatures of instinct, born only to be caught and destroyed, and like animals they too will perish.	10	Yet these people speak abusively against whatever they do not understand; and what things they do understand by instinct, like unreasoning animals–these are the very things that destroy them.
2:15	They have left the straight way and wandered off to follow the way of Balaam son of Bezer, who loved the wages of wickedness.	11	Woe to them! They have taken the way of Cain; they have rushed for profit into Balaam's error; they have been destroyed in Korah's rebellion.
2:13	They will be paid back with harm for the harm they have done. Their idea of pleasure is to carouse in broad daylight. They are blots and blemishes, revelling in their pleasures while they feast with you.	12	These people are blemishes at your love feasts, eating with you without the slightest qualm–shepherds who feed only themselves. They are clouds without rain, blown along by the wind; autumn trees, without fruit and uprooted–twice dead.
2:17	These people are springs without water and mists driven by a storm. Blackest darkness is reserved for them.	12–13	These people are blemishes at your love feasts, eating with you without the slightest qualm–shepherds who feed only themselves. They are clouds without rain, blown along by the wind; autumn trees, without fruit and uprooted–twice dead. They are wild waves of the sea, foaming up their shame; wandering stars, for whom blackest darkness has been reserved forever.
2:18	For they mouth empty, boastful words and, by appealing to the lustful desires of sinful human nature, they entice people who are just escaping from those who live in error.	16	These people are grumblers and faultfinders; they follow their own evil desires; they boast about themselves and flatter others for their own advantage
3:1–2	Dear friends, this is now my second letter to you. I have written both of them as reminders to stimulate you to wholesome thinking. I want you to recall the words spoken in the past by the holy prophets and the command given by our Lord and Saviour through your apostles.	17	But, dear friends, remember what the apostles of our Lord Jesus Christ foretold

3:3	Above all, you must understand that in the last days scoffers will come, scoffing and following their own evil desires.	18	They said to you, "In the last times there will be scoffers who will follow their own ungodly desires."

Similar Expressions[50]

2 Peter		Jude	
2:13	Blemishes	12	Blemishes
2:13	Feast with you	12	Eating with you
3:3	Scoffers	18	Scoffers

SELECTED BIBLIOGRAPHY

Bauckham, Richard J. *Jude, 2 Peter*. Vol. 50. WBC. Waco, TX: Word Books, 1983.

Baur, William. "Balaam." In *The International Standard Bible Encyclopedia*, edited by James Orr. Grand Rapids, MI: Eerdmans, 1915.

Bigg, Charles. *A Critical and Exegetical Commentary on the Epistles of St. Peter and St. Jude*. ICC. Edinburgh: T & T Clark, 1901.

Bray, Gerald L. *James, 1–2 Peter, 1–3 John, Jude*. ACCS. Downers Grove, IL: InterVarsity Press, 2000.

Carson, D. A. "Jude." In *Commentary on the New Testament Use of the Old Testament*, edited by G. K. Beale and D. A. Carson. Grand Rapids, MI: Baker Academic, 2007.

Charles, J. Daryl. "Jude." In *Expositor's Bible Commentary: Hebrews-Revelation*, edited by Tremper Longman III and David E. Garland. Revised edition. Grand Rapids, MI: Zondervan, 2012.

Charles, R. H., and W. O. E. Oesterley. *The Book of Enoch*. London: SPCK, 1917.

Fiensy, David A. *New Testament Introduction*. CPNIV. Joplin, MO: College Press, 1997.

Guthrie, Donald. *New Testament Introduction*. 4th revised edition. Downers Grove, IL: InterVarsity Press, 1996.

Hatfield, Lawson G. "Balaam." In *Holman Illustrated Bible Dictionary*, edited by Chad Brand, Archie England, and Charles W. Draper. Nashville, TN: Broadman & Holman, 2003.

House, H. Wayne. *Charts of Christian Theology and Doctrine*. Grand Rapids, MI: Zondervan, 1992.

Kato, Byang H. "Black Theology and African Theology." *Evangelical Review of Theology* 1 (1977): 35–48.

Kelly, J. N. D. *The Epistles of Peter and of Jude*. BNTC. London: Continuum, 1969.

Leaney, A. R. C. *The Letters of Peter and Jude: A Commentary*. Cambridge: Cambridge University Press, 1967.

Lucas, Dick, and Christopher Green. *The Message of 2 Peter & Jude*. BST. Downers Grove, IL: InterVarsity Press, 1995.

Metzger, Bruce M. *A Textual Commentary on the Greek New Testament*. 2nd edition. New York: United Bible Societies, 1994.

Mickelsen, A. Berkeley. "Eternal Life." In *Holman Illustrated Bible Dictionary*, edited by Chad Brand, Archie England, and Charles W. Draper. Nashville, TN: Broadman & Holman, 2003.

Moo, Douglas J. *2 Peter, Jude*. NIVAC. Grand Rapids: Zondervan, 1997.

Mounce, Bill. "Jesus Is Back in Jude." Accessed January 1, 2014. http://www.teknia.com/blog/jesus-back-jude.

Pink, Arthur W. *The Attributes of God*. Grand Rapids, MI: Baker Book House, 1975.

Schreiner, Thomas R. *1, 2 Peter, Jude*. Vol. 37. The New American Commentary. Nashville, TN: Broadman & Holman, 2003.

Wallace, Daniel B. *Greek Grammar Beyond the Basics: An Exegetical Syntax of the New Testament*. Grand Rapids: Zondervan, 1996.

ENDNOTES

2 Peter

1. Richard Bauckham, for example, argues that the apostle was not the author, and that those who received the letter would have been well aware of this because he was writing within the testamentary genre, where the use of an assumed name was common. So Bauckham argues that "the Petrine authorship was intended to be an entirely *transparent* fiction" *Jude, 2 Peter*, WBC (Waco, TX: Word, 1983), 134. Against this position, D. A. Carson and Douglas J. Moo argue that although 2 Peter is similar in style to a Jewish testament, "the overarching genre category to which 2 Peter belongs is the letter" (*An Introduction to the New Testament* [2nd ed.; Grand Rapids: Zondervan, 2005], 662). They rightly insist that there is no hint in the letter that the reference to the author's presence at the Mount of Transfiguration is not meant to be taken literally.

2. The table below sets out possible reasons for rejecting Peter's authorship of this letter and the counter-arguments of those who believe that Peter did write it. For more information about the former set of arguments, see Brevard S. Childs, *The New Testament as Canon: An Introduction* (Philadelphia: Fortress, 1985), 466–67. For more on the responses to the objections to Petrine authorship, see Carson and Moo, *An Introduction to the New Testament*, 661–663.

Arguments against Petrine authorship	Arguments in support of Petrine authorship
The differences between 1 and 2 Peter as regards style, vocabulary, and themes are so great that they cannot be explained by a simple change of amanuensis (scribe) or even audience but point to different authors. The Greek used and the erudite style are unlikely to come from an uneducated author who began life as a fisherman.	The Greek of 2 Peter is not as distinct as many scholars claim. Peter may have adopted a style his audience knew to create common ground with them. During his ministry in Asia Minor, Greece and Rome, Peter could easily have learnt superb Greek and an esteemed rhetorical style
The Apostle Peter would not have quoted Jude.	It is impossible to say whether Peter is quoting Jude or vice versa. Moreover, both Peter and Jude may have been quoting some other source.
The mention of Paul's letters as having similar authority to the OT Scripture suggests that this letter must have been written at a late date, when the NT canon had been compiled.	We do not know precisely when the NT books came to be considered canonical, and the apostles clearly considered that their words had an authority similar to that of Scripture (see 1 Cor 5:3; 2 Cor 10:11; 1 Thess 2:13; 2 Thess 2:15; 3:14). Moreover 3:15–16 does not have to imply that the works of the apostles were already collected as Scripture.

The reference to the passing of the first generation of Christians (3:4) suggest that this letter was written in the second-century, after the apostolic age.	The "fathers" referred to in 3:4 are not the first generation of Christians but are Abraham, Isaac, and Jacob, who were the ancestors of the Jewish nation (Luke 1:55, 72; Acts 3:13, 25).
The way in which the apostles are referred to in 3:2 suggests that the author is not himself an apostle.	Peter could be using the third person as a self-effacing way of referring to himself and the other apostles.
The writer warns against Gnosticism, which only became prominent in the second-century, and so this letter must have been written at that time.	The letter does not specify the exact nature of the heresy being addressed. Similar warnings are not uncommon in the NT.

3. Lee Martin McDonald observes that Peter's authorship of 1 Peter was not disputed in the early church:

> Although there are several parallel phrases in *Barnabas* and 1 Peter (*Barn.* 5.6 and 1 Pet 1:20), it is only with Polycarp that clear use of 1 Peter is found . . . The author of 2 Pet 3:1 . . . refers to the existence of an earlier letter by the Apostle Peter. Eusebius claimed that Papias (ca. 100–150) knew and used 1 Peter (*Hist. eccl.* 3.39.17), and he includes it in the list of the recognized books (3:25.2 and 3.3.1). Irenaeus was the first to use 1 Peter by name (*Haer.* 4.9.2; 4.16.5; 5.7.2), and thereafter many references are made to the book by the early church fathers. Early witnesses validate the use of the book in the church, and it does not appear to have been seriously questioned in the fourth century, even though it is missing in the Muratorian Fragment. (Lee Martin McDonald, *The Biblical Canon: Its Origin, Transmission, and Authority* [Grand Rapids: Baker Academic, 2007], 396)

4. The question of the authorship of 2 Peter is closely linked to its canonicity (the process by which the church recognized and compiled the books of the NT). It is true that the early church fathers quoted it less than they did other NT books. Origen (ca.184–253) is the first to explicitly cite 2 Peter, which he attributed to the Apostle Peter. The inclusion of this book in the canon continued to be debated until Athanasius of Alexandra, our African brother, set the stage for its acceptance in AD 376. However, the acceptance of 2 Peter as part of the canon was still being debated at the time of the Reformation. Martin Luther, for example, did not think that the gospel message shone through it (McDonald, *The Biblical Canon*, 396).

5. This type of arrangement of the material is referred to by scholars as a chiastic structure.

6. Carson and Moo, 654. The fact that this letter is bracketed or framed by the imperative form of *spoudazō* (make effort) (1:10; 3:14) and the nouns *gnōsis* (knowledge) (1:5, 6; 3:18), and *charis* (grace) (1:2 and 3:18) suggests that the writer is using the literary device known as inclusio.

7. J. L. Summey, "Adversaries" in *Dictionary of the Later New Testament and Its Developments* (ed. Ralph P. Martin and Peter H. Davids (Downers Grove, IL: InterVarsity, 1997), 29–30.

8. P. H. Davids, "2 Peter" in *New Dictionary of Biblical Theology*, ed. S. Rosner Brian et al. (Downers Grove, IL: InterVarsity, 2000).

9. In the Greek, Simon is spelled *Symeōn*, which is an alternative to the more usual spelling *Simōn* (W. Bauer, F. W. Danker, and F. W. Gingrich, eds., *A Greek-English Lexicon of the New Testament and Other Early Christian Literature*, BDAG (Chicago: University of Chicago Press, 2000), s.v. "Συμεών."

10. Steven L. Cox, "Peter" in *Holman Illustrated Bible Dictionary* eds. Chad Owen Brand, Charles W. Draper, and Archie W. England (Nashville: Holman, 2003), 1281–82.

11. Joseph Hart, "Come, Ye Sinners, Poor and Wretched," *Hymnal.net*, accessed December 1, 2013, http://www.hymnal.net/hymn.php/h/1032.

12. *BDAG*, s.v. "Δοῦλος"; J. P. Louw and Eugene A. Nida, eds., *Greek–English Lexicon of the New Testament: Based on Semantic Domains* (New York: United Bible Societies, 1988), s.v. "Δοῦλος."

13. Carson rightly argues that if we translate "apostle" simply as "messenger" the focus is entirely on the message to be conveyed. But as used in the NT the term "commonly bears the meaning a *special representative* or a *special messenger* rather than just 'someone sent out'" (D. A. Carson, *Exegetical Fallacies* [Grand Rapids: Baker, 1996], 30).

14. A. F. Walls, "Apostle" in *New Bible Dictionary*, ed. I. Howard Marshall et al. (Downers Grove, IL: InterVarsity, 1996), 58.

15. *BDAG*, s.v. "ἀπόστολος."

16. Thomas R. Schreiner, *1, 2 Peter, Jude,* NAC (Nashville, TN: Broadman & Holman, 2003), 276–277.

17. The only other usage of the word "faith" in this letter also has this subjective sense (see 2 Pet 1:5).

18. See *BDAG*, s.v. "λαγχάνω." The same word is used of Judas in Acts 1:17. There the KJV translates it as he "obtained part of this ministry" and the ESV as "was allotted his share in this ministry". The noun derived from the same root is used of choosing something by lot in Luke 1:9 and John 19:24.

19. J. Daryl Charles, "2 Peter" in *The Expositor's Bible Commentary: Hebrews–Revelation*, rev. ed. (Grand Rapids: Zondervan, 2006), 383.

20. In the Greek, "God" and "Saviour" are both modified by the same definite article. Thus, both terms apply to Jesus Christ.

21. The exalted status of Christ referred to in 2 Peter 1:1b is mentioned again in 2 Peter 3:18, highlighting his glory and framing the letter with references to the supremacy of Christ.

22. See also Leviticus 19:36; 22:33; 25:38; 26:13; Numbers 15:41; Deuteronomy 5:6; 6:12; 8:14; 13:5, 10; 2 Kings 17:36; Jeremiah 14:8.

23. The Greek verb in the phrase "be yours in abundance" (NIV) or "be multiplied" (ESV, NASB, KJV) is in the passive voice. It is an example of the divine passive construction, in which God is the one doing the action.

24. "Knowledge of God and of Jesus Christ" is both objective and subjective, meaning that the Father and the Son are the authors and content of this knowledge.

25. Scriptures marked NRSV throughout this book are from the New Revised Standard Version Bible, copyright © 1989 National Council of the Churches of Christ in the United States of America. Used by permission. All rights reserved.

26. Schreiner, *1, 2 Peter, Jude,* 288.

27. A literal translation of the original sentence might read "As all things to us His divine power (the things pertaining unto life and piety) hath given, through the acknowledgement of him who did call us through glory and worthiness, through which to us the most great and precious promises have been given, that through these ye may become partakers of a divine nature, having escaped from the corruption in the world in desires" (YLT). The "as" translates the particle *hōs*, which most English translations ignore because it is difficult to determine its function.

    Although the English translations treat the genitive participle *dedōrēmenēs* as the main verb, the construction in v. 3 is actually a genitive absolute introduced by the particle *hōs*. Some translators argue that this should be linked to v. 2, which would yield this translation "Grace to you and peace be multiplied in the knowledge of God and of Jesus our Lord; seeing that his divine power hath granted unto us all things that pertain unto life and godliness" (ASV; see also NASB). On this understanding, Christ's power is the basis for God's gift of grace and peace or the way in which God gives grace and peace. Osborne states "the 'grace and peace' provided by God (1:2) is anchored in his power for living (1:3)" (Grant R. Osborne, "2 Peter", in Grant R. Osborne and M. Robert Mulholland Jr., *James, 1 & 2 Peter, Jude, Revelation,* CBC [Carol Stream, IL: Tyndale House, 2011], 288).

    However, it is more likely that the genitive absolute in v. 3 should be linked to v. 4, for genitive absolutes usually precede the sentence they modify, rather than follow it. That is why the majority of translations, including the NIV, interpret verse 3 as explaining the manner of God's work in v. 4. In other words, God has given us his great and precious promises and, by so doing, he has granted us everything we need for life and godliness. In this interpretation, which is the one adopted in this commentary, the particle *hōs* expresses the manner of the action of *dedōrētai* in verse 4.

28. This is the only time the expression "divine power" occurs in the NT. The word rendered "divine" is used in the NT and OT (LXX) only for God (Exod 31:3; 35:31; Prov 2:17; Job 27:3; 33:4; Acts 17:29). The fact that word "power" as used in 1:16 clearly refers to Christ is a further indication that in v. 3 it is Christ who wields power (see Schreiner, 291).

29. *BDAG*, s.v. "εὐσέβεια" states that the NT and LXX use "godliness" to refer to "respect accorded to God in devout piety".

30. Scriptures marked ESV throughout this book are from The Holy Bible, English Standard Version® (ESV®), copyright © 2001 by Crossway, a publishing ministry of Good News Publishers. Used by permission. All rights reserved.

31. Those who argue that "him" refers to Christ base their argument on the fact that he is the object of knowledge in all the other occurrences of the term "knowledge" in this letter (1:2, 8; 2:20).

32. Here I am taking the dative phrase *idią doxę kai aretę* as a dative of advantage (see also Cleon L. Rogers Jr. and Cleon L. Rogers III, *The New Linguistic and Exegetical Key to the Greek New Testament* [Grand Rapids: Zondervan, 1998], 581).

33. Scriptures marked RSV throughout this book are from Revised Standard Version of the Bible, copyright © 1946, 1952, and 1971 National Council of the Churches of Christ in the United States of America. Used by permission. All rights reserved.

34. With this translation, the dative *idią doxę kai aretę* is interpreted as a dative of means, "used to indicate the means or instrument by which the verbal action is accomplished" (Daniel B. Wallace, *Greek Grammar Beyond the Basics: An Exegetical Syntax of the New Testament* [Grand Rapids: Zondervan, 1996], 162).

35. See also Osborne, 289. The relative pronoun translated "these" is in the genitive case although its antecedent is in the dative case because the preposition *dia* does not take the dative (Wallace, 368–9; *BDAG*, s.v. "διά").

36. See also Rogers and Rogers (581) who categorize this adjective as a superlative.

37. The RSV translates the last part of verse 4 as "escape the corruption that is in the world because of passion, and become partakers of the divine nature". But the conjunction "and" is not in the Greek, and the participle is not a full verb, which would make this an independent clause. The NIV translation "having escaped" is to be preferred.

38. The phrase *make every effort* is a participle in the Greek and could also be rendered "*applying* all zeal". This participle is not an attendant circumstance, although syntactically it could be argued to be such. However, semantically the action of the participle is not a necessary prelude to the action of the main verb. Rather, the action of the participle is the force by which the action of the main verb is carried out. It seems better to take it as a participle of means, stating how the action of the main verb is accomplished.

39. Charles comments on this as follows:

    That this verb appears three times in 2 Peter (vv. 5, 10, 15) is highly instructive . . .
    It reflects the seriousness of the community's situation as well as the pastoral strategy
    in addressing the readers. Theirs is the challenge of exhibiting moral character
    amidst pagan amoral culture. This requires willingness and determination, both of
    which at the present may be lacking. (p. 386)

40. Peter presents this list of virtues in a style that is not paralleled anywhere else in the NT, for each virtue is mentioned twice. The most similar lists would be Romans 5:3–5; Galatians 5:22–23; and James 1:3–4 (Bauckham, 184).

41. Osborne, 291.

42. Osborne suggests that there is a progression in Peter's list, "The verses in 2 Peter portray a very particular kind of virtue list called *sorites,* a chain list that proceeds step-by-step to a climax, with each one mentioned twice" (Osborne, 291). While this is a possibility, it is difficult to discern a clear step-by-step progression towards a climax. For example, it is difficult to see how knowledge builds on goodness. Rather, one would think that goodness should build on knowledge if the

list were in a particular order. There may be significance to the fact that the last virtue in the list is love, but not much can be said with regard to the order of the other virtues.

43. Schreiner, 300. He continues, "Moral restraint must be combined with endurance and steadfastness for those who hope to win the eschatological prize."

44. Charles observes, "while vice and virtue lists in the NT are not of the same compositional variety, one peculiar feature absent from pagan catalogues is the occasional movement toward crescendo or decrescendo" (Charles, 389).

45. Scott J. Hafemann, *The God of Promise and the Life of Faith: Understanding the Heart of the Bible* (Chicago: Crossway, 2001), 191.

46. Bauckham (189) argues that "near-sighted" and "blind" are synonyms, used together to increase the rhetorical effect.

47. *BDAG*, s.v. "βέβαιος."

48. John Calvin, *Calvin's Commentaries (Complete)*, trans. John King (Edinburgh: Calvin Translation Society, 1847), 340.

49. The conjunction "for" shows that verse 10b further explains 10a. "These things" refers to the list of virtues in 1:5–7.

50. The construction *ou mē* plus the subjunctive is the strongest emphatic negation in Greek.

51. The Greek does not include the conjunction "and" which introduces 1:11 in the NIV. It is best to translate this verse as "For in this way there will be richly provided for you an entrance into the eternal kingdom of our Lord and Saviour Jesus Christ." (ESV). The phrase "For in this way" connotes that it is through the practice of godliness (1:5–7) that we will be provided entrance into the kingdom.

52. Schreiner, 306.

53. The future tense in "will always remind you" should not be interpreted as suggesting that Peter intended to write another letter after 2 Peter.

> In fact, the use of the future tense with reference to the whole of the present letter, though unusual, is quite intelligible here. The apostle is represented as thinking not of the activity of writing the letter, but of the function that the letter will perform when he has written it. He intends the letter to be a *permanent* reminder of his teaching, not only to be read on one specific occasion, but to be available at all times (1:15). Thus even from the standpoint of his readers the letter's function of reminding continues into the future. So neither the epistolary aorist, which would imply that from the readers' standpoint the action of reminding is complete, nor the present tense, which would not convey the apostle's intention of writing for the future, would have been appropriate. (Bauckham, 195–6)

54. A literal translation would use the passive perfect participle here, "having been established". This divine passive designates God as the one who establishes us in the truth of the gospel.

55. The conjunction "for" at the beginning of 1:16 shows that 1:16–21 further explain the reason for the reminders that Peter is giving. In this section, he offers two more reasons for his repeated reminders.

56. This Greek term *parousia* (coming) could simply mean "presence" (see also 1 Cor 16:17; 2 Cor 10:10; Phil 2:12), but it is overwhelmingly used in the NT as a technical term for the second advent of Christ to judge the world and bring history to its close (Matt 24:3, 27, 37, 39; 1 Cor 15:23; 1 Thess 2:19; 3:13; 4:15; 5:23; 2 Thess 2:1; 8; Jas 5:7; 1 John 2:28). That is the way Peter seems to use it here.

57. The language of sonship used here also reminds us of the words of Psalm 2:7, which the NT writers quote several times as a proof text for Jesus being the Messiah (see also Acts 13:33; Heb 1:5; 5:5).

58. The Greek word used here can mean "sure", "certain", "reliable", or "firm" (see Rom 4:16; 2 Cor 1:7; Heb 2:2; 3:14; 6:19; 9:17; 2 Pet 1:10).

59. Scriptures marked NASB throughout this book are from the New American Standard Bible®, Copyright © 1960, 1962, 1963, 1968, 1971, 1972, 1973, 1975, 1977, 1995 by The Lockman Foundation. Used by permission.

60. So J. N. D. Kelly, *The Epistles of Peter and of Jude,* BNTC (Peabody, MA: Hendrickson, 1993), 321. Schreiner, however, argues that Peter is not referring to the entire OT Scripture but to the prophecies about the day of judgement and salvation (Schreiner, 319). While Schreiner's position is possible, it seems more likely that the reference is to the entire OT because of the generic reference to Scripture in 1:20 (see also Luke 24:27). This term *graphē*, translated "Scripture", occurs about fifty times in the NT and often refers to the OT in its entirety. The singular form with the definite article (*hēgraphē*) is used for specific passages of the OT cited in the NT (Mark 12:10; Luke 4:21; John 13:18; 19:24, 28, 36–37; Acts 1:16; 8:32, 35; Rom 4:3; 9:17; 10:11; 11:2; Gal 4:30; 1 Tim 5:18; Jas 2:8, 23; 4:5; 1 Pet 2:6). However, the singular *hēgraphē* is also used for OT Scripture as a whole when it is used in a context where there is no specific citation (John 2:22; 7:38, 42; 10:35; 17:12; 19:28; 20:9; Gal 3:8, 22; 2 Tim 3:16). The plural is used in a similar way: for specific OT passages with a quotation in context (Matt 21:42) and for the OT as a whole without a quotation from the OT (Matt 22:29; 26:54, 56; Mark 12:24; 14:49; Luke 24:27, 32, 45; John 5:39; Acts 17:2, 11; 18:24, 28; Rom 1:2; 15:4; 16:26; 1 Cor 15:3–4). The word *graphē* in 2 Peter 1:20, which occurs without reference to any particular OT passage, is thus likely referring to the OT as a whole.

61. The adjective *bebaios* could be a superlative (see Rogers and Rogers, 583).

62. Schreiner, 322.

63. Adapted from Paul Lee Tan, "Lawyer writing a promissory note for a horse he killed" in *Encyclopedia of 15,000 Illustrations* (Garland, TX: Bible Communications, 1996).

64. "The people" is a common way of referring to Israel in both the OT and NT (Exod 18:1; Lev 7:20; Deut 32:9; Ps 78:20; Matt 2:4; 26:47; 21:1; Luke 19:47; Acts 26:17).

65. Osborne lists seven characteristics of false prophets in the OT: (1) they practiced divination (Deut 18:9–14; see also Jer 14:14; Mic 3:7); (2) their prophecies were not fulfilled (1 Kgs 22:28; Isa 30:8; Jer 28:9); (3) they sought to please people instead of speaking for God (Jer 8:11; Mic 3:5, 11); (4) they lacked a word from God and thus were drawing people away from God (Deut 13:1–3; Jer 28:15; see also Amos 7:14–15); (5) they failed to uphold the Torah and to remain faithful to its regulations (Jer 6:10–15; 8:9–10); (6) they lacked authentication by miracles (1 Kgs 18); and (7) they lacked the moral character that would validate a true prophet – they lied (Jer 8:11); were drunk (Isa 28:7), and immoral (Jer 23:14) (Osborne, 310).

66. Osborne, 311–13.

67. The same word is used in the Septuagint translation of Genesis 34:10, 21; 42:34; Ezekiel 27:13; 2 Chronicles 1:16.

68. Bauckham notes "If it was the opponents themselves who suggested that God's judgment was idle or asleep, it is more relevant to note that these ideas were used by pagan sceptics to mock the inactivity of the gods who seem so rarely to intervene in the world" (Bauckham, 247–248).

69. 2 Peter 2:4–10a seems to have the following structure:
     A Former Condemnation (2:4–6)
     B Former Redemption (2:7–8)
     B′ Present Redemption (2:9a)
     A′ Future Condemnation (2:9b–10a)

70. 2 Peter 2:4–8 forms the long *protasis,* and 2:9–10a, the *apodosis.* There are three conditional clauses in the *protasis:* verses 4, 5, and 6. Verse 10 explains the consequence of these three conditions. In the Greek there is only one Greek conditional conjunction in verse 4 that governs all three statements.

71. One argument in favour of this position is the reference in 1 Peter 3:19 to the angels who did not obey in Noah's day and were imprisoned. Bauckham supports this view and argues that the sin of these angels is sexual indulgence.

     Those who (later) objected to the idea that angels could have mated with women did not suggest that the angels sinned in some other way, but that "the sons of God" in Gen 6:1 were not angels at all, but men. If the author of 2 Peter and his readers knew the story of the fall of the Watchers at all, they must have known it as an interpretation of Gen 6:1–4 and have known that the angels sinned by taking human wives. But instead of specifying the sins of each of his three OT examples of sinners in turn, the author has chosen to sum up the sins of all three in the words of v. 10a, which in fact give a strong emphasis to sexual indulgence (Bauckham, 248–249; see also Schreiner, 336; Robert B. Hughes and J. Carl Laney, *Tyndale Concise Bible Commentary* [Wheaton, IL: Tyndale House, 2001], 699).

While this position has much to commend it, it does not address the question of whether angels can have sex with human beings. Scripture in its entirety would seem to suggest that they cannot. It is true that we see the men of Sodom and Gomorrah attempting to have sex with the angels whom Yahweh sent to bring judgment on them (Gen 19:1–11), but they did not succeed. Moreover, Jesus' words in Matthew 22:30 imply that angels were not made for sexual relations: "At the resurrection people will neither marry nor be given in marriage; they will be like the angels in heaven" (Matt 22:30).

If "the sons of God" were not fallen angels, what were they? I argue that they were fallen angels who worked through men – in other words, they were demons who possessed men and then had sexual intercourse with women. VanGemeren supports this view:

> A modification of the angelic view is not impossible and deserves all consideration. In Hebrew the phrase "the Sons of God" may refer to any being, who is not man and not God. The language is not precise. They may be angels, demons, or one could even conceive of demon-possessed men who took to themselves wives, who were not possessed. (Willem A. VanGemeren, "The Sons of God in Genesis 6:1-4: An Example of Evangelical Demythologization?," *WTJ* 43, no. 2 [1981]: 348. See also Bruce K. Waltke, *Genesis: A Commentary* [Grand Rapids: Zondervan, 2001], 117)

72. Some may ask, "If demons are consigned to chains, how it is that they are still active in the world?" I suggest that only some of the fallen angels were chained – those who did not obey in Noah's day (1 Pet 3:18–19).

73. The Hebrew translated "wipe way" (*māḥā*) is used in other contexts to refer to the effect of God's wrath. It is also translated as "blot out" (Exod 32:32; Deut 9:14; 29:20; 2 Kgs 14:27; Ps 9:5).

74. Bauckham's argument that Noah was actually a preacher does not have clear biblical support. He bases his argument mainly on Jewish traditions (Bauckham, 250–51).

75. Some may wonder whether Noah is judged righteous because of his actions, and whether he is thus an example of works righteousness. Against this position, it can be argued that it is significant that Moses mentions Noah's righteousness (Gen 6:8–9) before talking about his acts of obedience (Gen 6:22; 7:5, 16). This order may suggest that it was not his deeds that made him righteous but the fact that he still had faith in God at a time when others had abandoned God. Noah was found to be righteous because of his faith, and this faith resulted in his being obedient to God's commands. That is why he is referred to as a man of faith in Hebrews 11:7.

76. God's covenant is only with Noah, as shown by the emphatic singular second person pronouns in Genesis 7:1 "*You, you yourself* [singular] enter, and all *your* house into the ark, for I have seen *you* (singular) righteous before this generation." But there are also recurrent references to those who were "with Noah" or "with him" (Gen 7:7, 9, 15, 23; 8:1, 16, 17, 18), suggesting that Noah's sons, wife, and the animals were saved because of their association with Noah. Just as the sin of the first Adam brought condemnation for those who were under him, so those who are under the new Adam, Noah, escape the judgement because Noah found favour with God (Gen 6:8–9).

77. Bauckham observes that "Noah, preserved from the old world to be the beginning of the new world after the Flood, is a type of faithful Christians who will be preserved from the present world to inherit the new world after the judgement" (Bauckham, 25).

78. Charles, 399.

79. Note that the word translated "trials" is singular in the Greek, and thus refers to affliction in general.

80. "For punishment" is a present participle in the Greek whose action is contemporaneous with the verb "to hold", suggesting that the wicked are presently enduring some punishment while God is keeping them for the Day of Judgment.

81. This does not militate against the truth that God does not want anyone to perish and does not take delight in the death of the wicked. In a sense, God can delight in one thing and will the

other. For more on how these two truths relate, see "Are There Two Wills in God" in John Piper, *The Pleasures of God: Meditations on God's Delight in Being God* (Sisters, OR: Multnomah Publishers, 2000), 313–40.

82. In Numbers 22:5, Balaam is identified as "the son of Beor", but in 2 Peter 2:15 Peter refers to him as "the son of Bezer" (Bosor [KJV, NET]). Some manuscripts attempted to clarify it by changing *Bezer* to *Beor*, following the Septuagint, but Bezer should be preferred as the more difficult reading. One manuscript has *Beōorsor*, which seems to be an amalgamation of *Bosor* and a marginal correction *eōr* (Metzger, 635). The word Peter chooses sounds like the Hebrew word for "flesh", and it could be that he was using a play on words to characterize Balaam and those who are now following him as belonging to the "flesh". Schreiner notes, "The word 'Bosor' likely derives from a pun on the word 'flesh' (*basar*) in Hebrew. Balaam was not a man of the Spirit but a man of the flesh. The false teachers, like Balaam, were not leading God's people in the righteous way but in the way of the flesh" (Schreiner, 354).

83. The Greek word translated "escape" in 2:18 is used in 1:4 to describe conversion (see also 2:20). Unbelievers are described as living in error in Romans 1:27, 2 Thessalonians 2:11 and 1 John 4:6.

84. The NASB best captures the Greek original: "Speaking out arrogant words of vanity they entice by fleshly desires" (see also NET, ESV). Their speeches are full of "meaningless words" (see 1 Tim 1:6; Titus 1:10).

85. The term also has a positive meaning: to simply "desire" something (see also Luke 22:15; Rev 18:14).

86. Schreiner, 357.

87. Verse 21 begins with "for" (omitted in the NIV), indicating that this is a continuation of the discussion.

88. In the Greek, the word translated "proverbs" is singular, implying that the two proverbs communicate the same thought.

89. The first occurrence of "beloved" in the Septuagint refers to Isaac (Gen 22:2, 12, 16), who prefigured Jesus, the beloved Son of God. In the Gospels "beloved" refers exclusively to Jesus (Matt 3:17; 12:18; 17:5; Mark 1:11; 9:7; 12:6; Luke 3:22; 20:13). In the rest of the NT, it is used of God's covenant people, Israel (Rom 11:28), specific believers (Acts 15:25; Rom 16:5, 8, 9, 12; 1 Cor 4:17; Eph 6:21; Col 1:7; 4:7, 9, 14; 1 Thess 2:8; 1 Tim 6:2; 2 Tim 1:2; Phlm 1:1, 16), and the church (Rom 1:7; 1 Cor 4:14; Eph 5:1; Jude 1:3; see also Rom 1:7; 12:19; 1 Cor 4:14; 1 Cor 10:14; 15:58; 2 Cor 7:1; 12:19; Eph 5:1; Phil 2:12; 4:1; Heb 6:9; Jas 1:16, 19; 2:5; 1 John 2:7; 3:2, 21; 4:1, 7, 11; 3 John 1:1; 1:2, 5, 11; Jude 1:3, 17, 20). In the Petrine corpus, Jesus is referred to as the beloved Son of God (1:17), and so are his servants, such as Paul (3:15) and all those who trust in the Son of God (3:1, 8, 14, 17). In fact, 2 Peter 3 is replete with the term "beloved" used with reference to faithful believers (3:1, 8, 14, 17) compared with a single occurrence elsewhere in the book, referring to Jesus (1:17).

90. We have no account of another authentic Petrine letter.

91. Some argue that the second person pronoun "your apostles" implies that this letter was not written by an apostle, and so was not written by Peter. However, it is more likely that the pronoun should be construed as "your apostles, namely, those who brought the gospel to you". See Schreiner, 371, and Bauckham, 289.

92. The Greek word *entolēs* (command) is used in various ways in the NT, but *BDAG* categorizes the usage in 3:2 under the meaning "God's expectations of Christians, with special reference to their ethical decisions" (*BDAG*, s.v. "ἐντολή").

93. Stephen D. Renn defines the last days as "the final period of human history before the consummation, resulting in eternal blessing for the righteous and condemnation for the wicked." *Expository Dictionary of Bible Words: Word Studies for Key English Bible Words Based on the Hebrew and Greek Texts* (Peabody, MA: Hendrickson, 2005, 577).

94. The NIV and ESV translate the dative here with a verbal sense ("scoffers will come, *scoffing*"). But this translation obscures Peter's focus on the nature of the scoffers rather than on their actions. I agree with those who argue that here the cognate dative is used in a way that is similar

to Hebrew expressions intended to intensify the meaning of a word, and so could better be translated as "blatant scoffers" (NET) or "barefaced scoffers".

95.   John 14:1–3; Acts 1:11; 1 Corinthians 15:23; 2 Corinthians 1:14; Philippians 1:6; 1 Thessalonians 3:13; 4:14–18; 2 Thessalonians 1:10; 2:1; 1 Timothy 6:14; 2 Timothy 4:8; Titus 2:13; Hebrews 9:28; James 5:7. The Greek term that is often used for this is *parousia*.

96.   The word used here would literally be translated as "fell asleep", which is a common euphemism for death (1 Kgs 2:10; 11:43; Matt 27:52; John 11:11; Acts 7:60; 13:36; 1 Cor 7:39), especially as it suggests the possibility of a later awakening at the resurrection (1 Cor 15:20; 1 Thess 4:14–15).

97.   Wallace suggests that the form of the verb represents a broad-band present tense that describes an action that began in the past and continues in the present, with emphasis on the present (Wallace, 519–20).

98.   Bauckham disagrees with this interpretation:

> If they are the OT fathers, then the argument of the scoffers must be that since the death of those to whom the promise of the *Parousia* of Jesus Christ was first given, in OT times through the OT prophets, everything has remained the same. This would be a general argument for the non-fulfilment of prophecy over the course of many centuries. Such an argument might be plausible in a purely Jewish context (see also 2 Apoc. Bar. 21:24), but it is an odd argument in an early Christian context. Early Christianity constantly argued that many OT prophecies, after remaining unfulfilled for centuries, had quite recently been fulfilled in the history of Jesus. The fulfilment of eschatological prophecy had begun and would be completed in the future with the fulfilment of those OT prophecies, which they held to be as yet unfulfilled. From this perspective it would not be very relevant to object that these prophecies had remained unfulfilled *since OT times*. Even if the false teachers denied that OT prophecies had been fulfilled in the life and work of Jesus, one would expect some reference to this fulfilment in 2 Peter's response. (Bauckham, 290)

> While Bauckham's argument is plausible, the fact that Peter goes back to creation and the flood, stating that these two key events were those that the false teachers forgot, suggests that "the fathers" may also reference to the OT patriarchs. Moreover, Peter had earlier called on the church to remember the predictions of the prophets, which suggests that it was those ancient predictions that were being twisted and despised by the scoffers.

99.   Although the phrase "by water" may suggest that water was the *agent* of creation, it must not be read that way. It seems best to interpret the clause as meaning that the world rose from and above water ("out of water") by God's word, see Murray J. Harris, *Prepositions and Theology in the Greek New Testament: An Essential Reference Resource for Exegesis* (Grand Rapids: Zondervan, 2012), 41.

100.   Schreiner, 376.

101.   The passive "are reserved" should be construed as a divine passive, meaning God is the one who is doing the reserving.

102.   See also Deuteronomy 32:22; Psalms 50:3; 97:3; Isaiah 30:30; 66:15–16; Ezekiel 38:22; Amos 7:4; Zephaniah 1:18; Malachi 4:1.

103.   Since Peter has been addressing believers all along – note the use of the second person pronoun in 3:1, 2, 8, 9 – it seems best to take the "you" as referring to believers here too.

104.   While the argument that God is patient for the sake of the elect may stand in the context of 2 Peter, there are other passages that are puzzling. Piper explains these passages well in an appendix entitled "Are There Two Wills in God?", in *The Pleasures of God: Meditations on God's Delight in Being God* (Sisters, OR: Multnomah, 1991), 313–40. Piper examines such passages as 1 Timothy 2:4, 2 Peter 2:9, and Ezekiel 18:23 and concludes that God's desire for all to be saved is not at odds with his sovereignty in electing grace. He argues that there are things that God would like to see happen, but that God actually wills something else to happen.

> There are "two wills in God" when it comes to salvation. They do not contradict. They are ordered according to God's infinite wisdom and one holds sway over the other when it is fitting in God's unfathomable mind ... It is God's supreme commitment to uphold and display the

full range of his glory through the sovereign demonstration [of] all his perfections, including his wrath and mercy, for the enjoyment of his chosen believing people (Piper, 339).

105. The Greek word translated "roar" is used only here in the New Testament and pertains to "noise made by something passing with a great force and rapidity" *BDAG*, s.v. "ῥοιζηδόν."

106. *BDAG*, s.v. "στοιχεῖον."

107. The pronoun rendered "What sort" instead of expressing a question, as in the NIV, hints at the greatness of the things that the apostle expects of believers (see also Rogers and Rogers, 589).

108. In the Greek, verses 11 and 12 form one long sentence. The translation used in the KJV preserves many details of its Greek text, but interprets the sentence as a question: "Seeing then that all these things shall be dissolved, what manner of persons ought ye to be in all holy conversation and godliness, looking for and hastening unto the coming of the day of God, wherein the heavens being on fire shall be dissolved, and the element shall melt with fervent heat?" The NIV retains the question form, but breaks the sentence in two. The NASB is closer to the Greek in its translation: "Since all these things are to be destroyed in this way, what sort of people ought you to be in holy conduct and godliness, looking for and hastening the coming of the day of God, because of which the heavens will be destroyed by burning, and the elements will melt with intense heat!" (see also ESV, NKJV, NET, RSV). It seems best to take these verses as an expectation expressed in an exclamation to show the apostle's eagerness.

109. Note that the day of judgement is called the "day of God" in 3:12 and "the day of Christ" elsewhere in the letter (1:16; 3:4). The fact that Peter uses "God" and "Christ" interchangeably shows that there is no doubt in his mind that Jesus Christ is God (see also 2 Pet 1:1; Titus 2:13).

110. The present tense of the Greek verbs in this sentence is taken as a futuristic present tense.

111. For more on this, see comments on 3:1.

112. The "these" in 3:14 refers back to the new heaven and new earth.

113. See also Exodus 34:9; Numbers 14:18; Nehemiah 9:17; Psalms 86:15; 103:8; 145:8; Jeremiah 15:15; Joel 2:13; Jonah 4:2; Nahum 1:3.

114. Peter's audience had probably seen some of Paul's letters addressed to other churches.

115. In the Greek the antecedent to the relative pronoun "which" is "some things hard to understand". Peter is not saying everything in Paul's letters is difficult to understand; only that some things are hard to grasp.

116. Charles Biggs says, "Scripture is the voice of the Spirit of Christ speaking through man (1 Pet 1:11), that Spirit which St. Paul claims as his teacher (1 Cor 2:12, 13), and by which his σοφία [wisdom] was given … Writing inspired by the Holy Spirit was 'holy writing,' and was afterwards canonised, because it had from the first been so considered. The Pauline Epistles were read in church, and even in churches to which they were not addressed (Col. 4:16; 1 Thess. 5:27), just as scripture was." (Charles Bigg, *A Critical and Exegetical Commentary on the Epistles of St. Peter and St. Jude*, ICC [Edinburgh: T & T Clark, 1901], 302).

    Another possible way of interpreting Peter's words, "as they do other Scriptures", is that it distinguishes Paul's letters from Scripture. This line of thought would translate the phrase as "the Scripture as well", or "the Scriptures on the other hand". These translations would distinguish Paul's letters from the Scriptures and not equate them. While possible, this line of reasoning is not supported by the text. The simplest reading of the Greek, *hōs kai*, is that it is a comparative, "as also the rest of Scriptures" (author's translation) or "as they do the other Scriptures".

117. The Greek participle translated "have been forewarned" is taken as a participle of ground, which states the reason for the command to be on guard.

118. Michael Green notes:

    The word for "steadfastness" (NIV *secure position*) *stērigmos,* occurs only here in the New Testament, but is from the same root as the verb Jesus had used in Luke 22:32, "When you have turned back, strengthen (*stērixon*) your brothers". This is a command which, throughout this Epistle, Peter has been seeking to obey. It is not surprising that he who had been so mercurial and had been changed by the grace of God into a man of rock should be so concerned about stability." (Michael Green, 2 *Peter and Jude: An Introduction and Commentary*, TNTC [Downers Grove, IL: InterVarsity, 1987], 174–75.)

119. Note that those who irreversibly fall away prove that they were never genuinely saved (1 John 2:19).

120. Schreiner (401–402) puts it this way:

    Doxologies that are clearly directed to Jesus Christ seldom occur in the NT, though 2 Tim 4:18 and Rev 1:5–6 are doxologies to Christ. A doxology to Christ constitutes another way that the letter is framed, for we already saw in 1:2 that Peter identified Jesus Christ as God and Saviour. Doxologies, of course, are only directed to God himself, and so the deity of Jesus Christ is communicated in the doxology.

121. Consider reading John Piper, "Why God Inspired Hard Texts," in *Brothers, We Are Not Professionals: A Plea to Pastors for Radical Ministry* (Nashville, TN: Broadman & Holman, 2002), 97–104.

Jude

1. Jerry L. Sumney, "Adversaries" in *Dictionary of the Later New Testament and Its Developments*, ed. Ralph P. Martin and Peter H. Davids (Downers Grove, IL: InterVarsity, 1997). For more on this question, see Appendix 1, which also sets out the parallels between 2 Peter and Jude.

2. Matthew 10:4; 26:14, 47; 27:3; Mark 3:19; 14:10, 43; Luke 6:16; 22:3, 47, 48; John 6:71; 12:4; 13:2, 26; 13:29; 18:2–3, 5; Acts 1:16, 25.

3. The letter is included in the Muratorian canon and Tertullian and Clement of Alexandria consider it canonical. "Eusebius (*H.E.* 2.23.25; 3.25.3) lists Jude among the 'contested' writings, but the doubts that existed were probably due to the references to noncanonical writings in the letter rather than to a contrary tradition" (Carson and Moo, 691). Nevertheless, some scholars still dispute Jude's authorship, arguing for an unknown Jude or that the letter is pseudonymous (see A. R. C. Leaney, *The Letters of Peter and Jude: A Commentary* [Cambridge: Cambridge University Press, 1967], 83).

    Three arguments are usually advanced against Jude, the Lord's brother, being the author. First, it is argued that the Greek is too good to have been written by a Galilean. This argument is weak, in that we cannot attempt to measure Jude's knowledge of Greek when we do not know him personally. Moreover, the fact that he is Galilean does not mean he could not have known good Greek. Second, it is argued that the reference to the apostle's teaching and the faith that was once for all entrusted to the saints imply a late date, when the apostolic writings were accepted as the standard for orthodoxy. But Jude 17 does not refer to a body of collected writings but to the predictions of Jesus and the apostles about the last days. Also the text does not require that the apostles mentioned have already died. Bauckham rightly argues "It is not the apostles themselves, but their missionary activity in founding these particular churches, which belongs to the past" (Bauckham, 13). Third, it is argued that if Jude the author was really the brother of the Lord, he would have mentioned that relationship in his epistle. However, the fact that the brothers of Jesus gained prominence in the early church lends credence to the idea that Jude, the Lord's brother, is the author. If the letter were being written under an assumed name, the writer would probably have mentioned Jude's relationship to Jesus to enhance the acceptance of his letter (Carson and Moo, 692). Since these arguments are weak, the argument for Jude the brother of Jesus as author stands.

4. Quoted in Gerald L. Bray, *James, 1-2 Peter, 1-3 John, Jude*, ACCS (Downers Grove, IL: InterVarsity, 2000), 245.

5. In place of "who are loved" the KJV has "them that are sanctified." The difference stems from a different spelling in the Greek. Good and very early Greek manuscripts support the reading "who are loved" while Byzantine manuscripts with some minuscules support the KJV reading. It seems likely that the KJV reading was introduced by scribes who were trying to avoid the difficulty of saying that someone is loved in God the Father, a concept that is not common in the New Testament (compare, Bruce M. Metzger, *A Textual Commentary on the Greek New Testament.,*

6. 2nd ed. [New York: United Bible Societies, 1994], 656). The New Testament mainly teaches that believers are loved and graced by God in Christ Jesus.

6. H. Wayne House, *Charts of Christian Theology and Doctrine* (Grand Rapids: Zondervan, 1992), 102.

7. These translations take the Greek dative "*Iēsou Christō*" as dative of advantage. But the KJV takes it as a dative of location and the HCSB and NET translate it as a dative of means.

8. Arthur W. Pink, *The Attributes of God* (Grand Rapids: Baker, 1975), 81.

9. Schreiner, 432.

10. Byang H. Kato, "Black Theology and African Theology," *EvRT* 1 (1977): 45–46.

11. Ibid., 47.

12. Ibid.

13. Acts 15:25; Romans 11:28; 12:19; 16:5, 8–9, 12; 1 Corinthians 4:14, 17; 10:14; 15:58; 2 Corinthians 7:1; 12:19; Ephesians 5:1; 6:21; Philippians 2:12; 4:1; Colossians 1:7; 4:7, 9, 14; 1 Thessalonians 2:8; 1 Timothy 6:2; 2 Timothy 1:2; Philemon 1:1, 16; Hebrews 6:9; James 1:16, 19; 2:5; 1 Peter 2:11; 4:12; 2 Peter 3:1, 8, 14–15, 17; 1 John 2:7; 3:2, 21; 4:1, 7, 11; 3 John 1:1–2, 5, 11; Jude 1:3, 17, 20.

14. The word "God" is not in the Greek, but is implicit in the divine passive "entrusted". For more on divine passives, see Wallace, 437–38.

15. *BDAG*, s.v. "ἅγιος."

16. Some Greek manuscripts have "they deny Jesus Christ our only Sovereign God and Lord", highlighting the divinity of Christ more clearly.

17. J. N. D. Kelly, *The Epistles of Peter and of Jude*, BNTC (London: Continuum, 1969), 254.

18. The ESV reflects the 28th edition of the Nestle Aland *Novum Testamentum Graece* (NA28). In other versions like the NIV, the variant reading "Jesus" is sometimes mentioned in a footnote. For an article in which Bill Mounce celebrates this translation, see "Jesus Is Back in Jude, http://www.teknia.com/blog/jesus-back-jude (accessed Nov 21, 2016).

19. See my comment on 2 Peter 2:4, where I suggest that the angels did not have direct sexual relationships with the daughters of men, but rather possessed men as demons do and worked through them.

20. See also D. A. Carson, "Jude", in *Commentary on the New Testament Use of the Old Testament*, eds. G. K. Beale and D. A. Carson (Grand Rapids: Baker, 2007), 1070.

21. Carson suggests that the celestial beings are unlikely to be evil angels:

> The verb for "slander" (*blasphēmeō*) has to do with dishonoring or shaming someone, speaking insultingly about someone, or the like. Angels sometimes are seen as the guardians of God's established order and thus his authority, or the ones who have mediated God's revelation to us (e.g. Acts 7:38, 53; 1 Cor 11:10; Heb. 2:2). To "slander" them, then, looks like rebellion against God's authority, which not only admirably fits the context but also is in line with the rebellious tendencies of the false teachers. (Carson, "Jude," 1074)

> While this argument seems convincing, the example that Jude gives in the following verse militates against this view. It seems best to match the "celestial beings" with the devil that the archangel Michael did not dare to rebuke (v. 9).

22. Schreiner, 457–58.

23. As far as we can judge, the dispute may have arisen because Satan claimed that Moses' body belonged to him because Moses had sinned and so had been denied entry to the promised land.

24. Richard J. Bauckham, *Jude, 2 Peter*, vol. 50, WBC (Waco, TX: Word Books, 1983), 60; Dick Lucas and Christopher Green, *The Message of 2 Peter & Jude*, BST (Downers Grove, IL: InterVarsity, 1995), 192–93; Douglas J. Moo, *2 Peter, Jude*, NIVAC (Grand Rapids: Zondervan, 1997), 246.

25. The NIV does not translate the conjunction *hoti* [for] that signals that their behaviour is the reason for their woe. The ESV is to be preferred: "for they walked in the way of …" (see also, NASB, NET and RSV).

26. It is very unlikely that Jude is presenting Cain as a false teacher, as Bauckham argues (79–80).

27. See Lawson G. Hatfield, "Balaam", in *Holman Illustrated Bible Dictionary,* eds. Chad Brand, Archie England, and Charles W. Draper (Nashville, TN: Broadman & Holman, 2003); William Baur, "Balaam", in *The International Standard Bible Encyclopedia*, ed. James Orr (Grand Rapids: Eerdmans, 1915).

28. The aorist rendered "have been destroyed" (*apo lonto*) is a futuristic or proleptic aorist. Wallace describes this use of the aorist as follows:

> The aorist *indicative* can be used to describe an event that is not yet past as though it were already completed. This usage is not at all common, though several exegetically significant texts involve possible proleptic aorists ... An author sometimes uses the aorist for the future to stress the certainty of the event. It involves a "rhetorical transfer" of a future event as though it were past. (Wallace, 563–64)

29. The phrase "love feasts" translates the plural *tais agapais*, the only instance of the plural of *agapē* (love) in the New Testament and Septuagint. The BDAG and all popular English translations render it as "love feasts" or something with similar meaning (see ESV, NASB, NIV 2011, NKJV, NET, NLT, CSB, NRSV).

30. Schreiner, 467. See also Kelly, 273.

31. Once again we have a divine passive, as the passive perfect tense "has been reserved" assumes God as the subject.

32. It is uncertain who authored this book. For more on its authorship see R. H. Charles and W. O. E. Oesterley, *The Book of Enoch* (London: SPCK, 1917), xv–xvii.

33. Charles observes,

> Given the Jewish-Christian character of the epistle, it is possible – indeed, most likely – that Jude's readers are products of a distinctly Palestinian religious-cultural milieu. Thus allusion to a popular sectarian Jewish work, while not necessarily viewed by Jude as "inspired," nevertheless is cited strategically for "inspired" usage, i.e. to suit Jude's particular theological/pastoral purpose. (J. Daryl Charles, "Jude", in *Expositor's Bible Commentary: Hebrews-Revelation*, eds. Tremper Longman III and David E. Garland, rev. ed. [Grand Rapids: Zondervan, 2012], 562.)

34. Scriptures marked HCSB are from the Holman Christian Standard Bible®, Copyright © 1999, 2000, 2002, 2003, 2009 by Holman Bible Publishers. Used by permission. Holman Christian Standard Bible®, Holman CSB®, and HCSB® are federally registered trademarks of Holman Bible Publishers.

35. Bauckham, 99.

36. The Greek phrase used here is a translation of a Hebrew expression that literally means "to lift up", and does not always have the bad connotation it has in Jude (see Gen 19:21; 32:20; 1 Sam 25:35).

37. The reference to the apostles should not be taken as implying that Jude wrote long after the apostles had died. That conclusion is not necessary based on the text as it stands. Jude simply adds his own voice to that of the apostles by reminding his readers of what they said (see Kelly, 281–82).

38. In other words, the genitive is either subjective or objective.

39. See also Schreiner, 483–84.

40. Note that the NIV translates v. 20 very well as it preserves the participles in the English (see also ESV, NET, NASB, ASV). But in the NIV translation of v. 21, however, it is not very clear that "wait" is also a participle. The RSV, NIV '84, and NLT treat all the participles as imperatives: build, pray, wait.

41. "Eternal life" is the future phase (Mark 10:30; John 12:25; Gal 6:8) of the present redemption (John 3:36; 5:24; 6:54). According to Jesus, eternal life is knowing the true God and Jesus, whom he sent (John 17:3). "Eternal life is given by Jesus and the Holy Spirit. This future reality, already experienced to some limited degree in the present, involves the Father, Son, and Spirit. Fellowship in life eternal means fellowship with the triune God." (A. Berkeley Mickelsen, "Eternal Life", in *Holman Illustrated Bible Dictionary* [Nashville, TN: Broadman & Holman, 2003]).

42. See Schreiner, 481–82.

43. These verses have a few textual issues, the most important of which is the difference between the shorter and longer reading. According to the shorter reading (in which *hous de eleate* is omitted and *enphobō* transposed), only two groups are addressed, whereas the longer reading mentions three groups. The longer text is to be preferred because it is strongly supported by several good early manuscripts (see also Metzger, 661). Moreover, the three groups listed here would match Jude's triplets, in verses 20–21.

44. *BDAG*, s.v. "ἁρπάζω."

45. Luke 2:11; John 4:42; Acts 5:31; 13:23; Ephesians 5:23; Philippians 3:20; 2 Timothy 1:10; Titus 1:4; 2:13; 3:6; 2 Peter 1:1, 11; 2:20; 3:2, 18; 1 John 4:14.

46. Schreiner, 492.

47. Charles Bigg, *A Critical and Exegetical Commentary on the Epistles of St. Peter and St. Jude*, ICC (Edinburgh: T & T Clark, 1901), 216–24; David A. Fiensy, *New Testament Introduction*, CPNIV (Joplin, MO: College Press, 1997), 349–50.

48. All these points are from David A. Fiensy and Donald Guthrie. For an extensive discussion of all the views I have mentioned, see Donald Guthrie, *New Testament Introduction*, 4th rev. ed. (Downers Grove, IL: InterVarsity, 1996), 916–24.

49. Schreiner (415–19) also argues for 2 Peter's dependence on Jude. See also J. N. D. Kelly, 225–27.

50. The links between these words are even clearer in the original Greek.

9 781783 684601